MODERN
POLITICAL
ANALYSIS

PRENTICE-HALL FOUNDATIONS OF MODERN POLITICAL SCIENCE SERIES

Robert A. Dahl, Editor

PRENTICE-HALL FOUNDATIONS OF MODERN POLITICAL SCIENCE SERIES

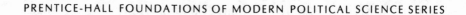

PRENTICE-HALL, INC., Englewood Cliffs, New Jersey

MODERN POLITICAL ANALYSIS

Third Edition

ROBERT A. DAHL

Yale University

Library of Congress Cataloging in Publication Data

Dahl, Robert Alan, (date)
   Modern political analysis.

   (Prentice-Hall foundations of modern political science series)
   Bibliography: p. 148
   Includes index.
   1. Power (Social sciences)   2. Political science.
I. Title.
JC330.D34 1976   320   75-35768
ISBN 0-13-596981-6 pbk.
ISBN 0-13-596999-9

PRENTICE-HALL FOUNDATIONS OF MODERN POLITICAL SCIENCE SERIES

Robert A. Dahl, Editor

MODERN POLITICAL ANALYSIS, Third Edition
by Robert A. Dahl

PRENTICE-HALL   INTERNATIONAL,   INC.,   London

PRENTICE-HALL   OF   AUSTRALIA,   PTY.   LTD.,   Sydney

PRENTICE-HALL   OF   CANADA,   LTD.,   Toronto

PRENTICE-HALL OF INDIA PRIVATE LIMITED, New Delhi

PRENTICE-HALL   OF   JAPAN,   INC.,   Tokyo

PRENTICE-HALL OF SOUTHEAST ASIA PTE. LTD., Singapore

10 9 8 7 6 5 4 3 2 1

CONTENTS

PREFACE

As you may have discovered, there are enthusiasts who appear to believe that most (if not all) important knowledge about politics can be found between the covers of a single book—or at least in the works of one author. If one studies my man X deeply enough, an enthusiast will say, one will find that he tells everything. The enthusiast's oracle most likely is some great name—Plato, Aristotle, Machiavelli, or Marx. But the oracle might turn out to be an ex-sportswriter, turned political pundit. I am reasonably sure that the search for a political oracle is in vain. For, I believe, it is a melancholy fact that no one has ever been wise enough to contribute more than a small fraction of what is known about politics.

Our enthusiast has a first cousin who insists that everything important has already been said in the great works of the past, as if wisdom, like wine, must be aged to make it better. Yet one may search long and hard in the great works and will not, I am quite sure, find as much about the operation of modern political parties, the American Congress, the political system of the USSR, or a great number of other topics, as one will find in recent studies.

For political institutions change. Modern democracy simply is not equivalent to the Athenian political system or the Roman Republic. Also, the study of politics to some extent is cumulative. Indeed, on certain topics, knowledge increases almost annually. If someone were to ask, "How can I learn about what sorts of people participate most in politics, and why?" I would urge him to start with the most recent studies in the field and work back. I seriously doubt that he would get much help from Aristotle, Rousseau, or the *Federalist Papers*.

Yet, I feel it is equally arrogant to suppose that very little worth knowing is to be found outside the more recent works. Recent studies often help us to gain a better judgment on questions of fact—and anyone who is contemptuous of fact had better forget about studying politics. Twenty-five centuries of dedicated study of politics naturally have produced many highly plausible but, unfortunately, contradictory hypotheses. Each can be strongly supported by common sense and can be argued till Doomsday as long as one sticks to the older methods of analysis. Happily, new methods of inquiry of analysis sometimes help us to settle these questions. Yet all the questions never do get answered and probably never will. The best of the profound works of the past, even of the distant past, make us aware of what these unanswered questions are. And they present us with the best fruits of creative minds struggling to arrive at answers. We do not know so much today that we can afford to neglect this older wisdom.

Now what, you ask, have these observations to do with a book on modern political analysis? This: Like the series of which it is a part, this book does not pretend to tell you all that you need to know about politics. Its aim is more modest but more realistic: to equip you with a few basic concepts, ideas, and analytical tools—ancient or recent, whichever seem better—so you can proceed more competently toward what should be, in a democracy, a life-long vocation: the analysis of politics.

A new chapter has been added to this edition—"What is Political Analysis?" (Chapter Two). In it I have sought to clarify four major orientations toward political understanding and action: searching for empirical knowledge, arriving at standards of evaluation, discovering policies designed to satisfy our standards of evaluation in the light of our empirical knowledge, and clarifying the meaning of our terms and concepts. I have also revised Chapter Three, "Political Influence," and I have expanded some concluding remarks into a new chapter (Chapter Four) on the different forms of influence.

In addition to my debts to the numerous scholars whose work makes a book like this possible—only a few of whom are cited—I should also like to acknowledge the help I have received from critics of the previous editions. I am also indebted to a number of people who read and commented on the original manuscript for this new edition, including several graduate students in my seminars at Yale. Finally, I want to thank Mrs. Nancy Hoskins for typing and editorial assistance.

Robert A. Dahl

MODERN
POLITICAL
ANALYSIS

CHAPTER ONE

WHAT
IS
POLITICS?

NATURE OF THE POLITICAL ASPECT

What distinguishes the political aspect of human society from other aspects? What are the characteristics of a political system as distinct, say, from an economic system? Although students of politics have never entirely agreed on answers to these questions, they tend to agree on certain key points. Probably no one would quarrel with the notion that a political system is a pattern of political relationships. But what is a political relationship?[1]

On this question, as on many others, an important, though not always entirely clear, place to start is Aristotle's *Politics* (written ca. 335–332 B.C.). In the first book of the *Politics*, Aristotle argues against those who say that all kinds of authority are identical and seeks to distinguish the authority of the political leader in a political association, or polis, from other forms of authority, such as the master over the slave, the husband over the wife, and the parents over the children.

Aristotle takes for granted, however, that at least one aspect of a political association is the existence of *authority* or *rule.* Indeed, Aristotle defines the polis, or political association, as the "most sovereign and inclusive association" and a constitution, or polity, as "the organization of a polis, in respect of its offices generally, but especially in respect of

---

[1]For a brief discussion of recent views on the scope of political science, see Oran R. Young's companion volume in this series, *Systems of Political Science,* Chapter One.

Figure 1

that particular office which is sovereign in all issues."[2] One of Aristotle's criteria for classifying constitutions is the portion of the citizen body in which final *authority* or *rule* is located.

Ever since Aristotle's time, the notion has been widely shared that a political relationship in some way involves authority, ruling, or power. For example, one of the most influential modern social scientists, the German scholar Max Weber (1864–1920), postulated that an association should be called political "if and in so far as the enforcement of its order is carried out continually within a given territorial area by the application and threat of physical force on the part of the administrative staff." Thus, although Weber emphasized the territorial aspect of a political association, like Aristotle he specified that a relationship of authority or rule was one of its essential characteristics.[3]

To take a final example, a leading contemporary political scientist, Harold Lasswell, defines "political science, as an empirical discipline, [as]

[2]Ernest Barker, ed., *The Politics of Aristotle* (New York: Oxford University Press, 1962), pp. 1, 110.

[3] *The Theory of Social and Economic Organization,* trans. A. M. Henderson and Talcott Parsons (New York: Oxford University Press, 1947), pp. 145–153, 154.

the study of the shaping and sharing of power" and "a political act [as] one performed in power perspectives."[4]

The areas of agreement and disagreement in the positions held by Aristotle, Weber, and Lasswell on the nature of politics are illustrated by Figure 1. Aristotle, Weber, and Lasswell, and almost all other political scientists agree that political relationships are to be found somewhere within circle A, the set of relationships involving power, rule, or authority. Lasswell calls everything in A political, by definition. Aristotle and Weber, on the other hand, define the term "political" so as to require one or more additional characteristics, indicated by circles B and C. For example, to Weber the domain of the political would not be everything inside A or everything inside B (territoriality) but everything in the area of overlap, AB, involving both rule *and* territoriality. Although Aristotle is less clear than either Weber or Lasswell on the point, doubtless he would limit the domain of the political even further—e.g., to relationships in associations capable of self-sufficiency (C). Hence, to Aristotle, "politics" would be found only in the area ABC.

Clearly, everything that Aristotle and Weber would call political, Lasswell would too. But Lasswell would consider as political some things that Weber and Aristotle might not: a business firm or a trade union, for example, would have "political" aspects. Let us therefore boldly define a political system as *any persistent pattern of human relationships that involves, to a significant extent, control, influence, power, or authority.*[5]

THE UBIQUITY OF POLITICS

Admittedly, this definition is very broad. Indeed, it means that many associations that most people ordinarily do not regard as "political" possess political systems: private clubs, business firms, labor unions, religious organizations, civic groups, primitive tribes, clans, perhaps even families. Three considerations may help clarify the unfamiliar notion that almost every human association has a political aspect:

(1) In common parlance we speak of the "government" of a club, a firm, and so on. In fact, we may even describe such a government as dictatorial, democratic, representative, or authoritarian; and we often hear about "politics" and "politicking" going on in these associations.

---

[4]Harold D. Lasswell and Abraham Kaplan, *Power and Society* (New Haven: Yale University Press, 1950), pp. xiv, 240.

[5]In Chapter Three, words like control, power, influence, and authority are called *influence-terms.* The concept of influence is defined in that chapter.

(2) A political system is only *one* aspect of an association. When we say that a person is a doctor, or a teacher, or a farmer, we do not assume that he is *only* a doctor, *only* a teacher, *only* a farmer. No human association is exclusively political in all its aspects. People experience many relationships other than power and authority: love, respect, dedication, shared beliefs, and so on.

(3) Our definition says virtually nothing about human *motives*. It definitely does not imply that in every political system people are driven by powerful inner needs to rule others, that leaders passionately want authority, or that politics is inherently a fierce struggle for power. Conceivably, relationships of authority could exist even among people of whom none had a passion for power, or in situations where people who most ardently thirsted for authority had the least chance of acquiring it. Thus the Zuni Indians of the American Southwest are reported to have had a very strong sense that power-seeking was illicit and power-seekers must not be given power.[6] Closer to our own experience is the not uncommon view among members of various American private organizations that those who want most intensely to head the organization are least suited to do so, while the most suitable are among those who least want the job. But whatever the evidence from anthropology or folklore may be, the central point is this: our highly general definition of a political system makes practically no assumptions as to the nature of human motives. Despite its breadth, the definition helps us make some critical distinctions that are often blurred in ordinary discussions.

Politics and Economics

Political analysis deals with power, rule, or authority. Economics concerns itself with scarce resources or the production and distribution of goods and services. Politics is one aspect of a great variety of human institutions; economics is another aspect. Hence an economist and a political scientist might both study the same concrete institution—the Federal Reserve system, for example, or the budget. But the economist would be concerned primarily with problems involving scarcity and the use of scarce resources, and the political scientist would deal primarily with problems involving relationships of power, rule, or authority. Like most distinctions between subjects of intellectual inquiry, however, that between politics and economics is not perfectly sharp.

Political Systems and Economic Systems

Many people indiscriminately apply terms like "democracy," "dictatorship," "capitalism," and "socialism" to both political and economic systems. This tendency to confuse political with economic systems stems

[6] Ruth Benedict, *Patterns of Culture* (Boston: Houghton Mifflin Co., 1934).

from the lack of a standardized set of definitions, from ignorance of the historical origins of these terms, and in some cases from a desire to exploit a highly favorable or unfavorable political term like "democracy" or "dictatorship" in order to influence attitudes toward economic systems.

It follows, however, that the political aspects of an institution are not the same as its economic aspects. Historically, the terms "democracy" and "dictatorship" usually have referred to political systems, whereas "capitalism" and "socialism" have referred to economic institutions. From the way the terms have been used historically, the following definitions are appropriate:

1. A democracy is a political system in which the opportunity to participate in decisions is widely shared among all adult citizens.
2. A dictatorship is a political system in which the opportunity to participate in decisions is restricted to a few.
3. Capitalism is an economic system in which most major economic activities are performed by privately owned and controlled firms.
4. Socialism is an economic system in which most major activities are performed by agencies owned by the government or society.

Each pair of terms, democracy–dictatorship, capitalism–socialism, implies a dichotomy, and dichotomies are often unsatisfactory. In fact, many political systems are neither wholly democratic nor wholly dictatorial; in many countries private and governmental operations are mixed together in all sorts of complex ways. These mixtures not only demonstrate the shortcomings of the dichotomy "capitalism–socialism" but also emphasize the fact that some institutions and processes can be viewed as part of the economic system for certain purposes and as part of the political system for others. The point to remember is that in spite of, or even because of, this intermixing it has proved to be intellectually fruitful to distinguish some aspects of life as "economic" and other aspects as "political."

Systems and Subsystems

Any collection of elements that interact in some way with one another can be considered a system: a galaxy, a football team, a legislature, a political party.[7] In thinking about political systems, it is helpful to keep in mind four points that apply to any system:

[7]The reader should consult Young, *Systems of Political Science*, Chapters Two and Three, for a discussion of definitions of the term "system," the nature of general systems theory, and the utility of the systems approach in political science. The most extensive attempt to apply systems theory to political science is in two works by David Easton: *A Framework for Political Analysis* (Englewood Cliffs, N.J.: Prentice-Hall, 1965) and *A Systems Analysis of Political Life* (New York: John Wiley & Sons, 1965).

(1) To call something a system in an abstract way (or, as some scholars say, an analytic way) of looking at concrete things. One therefore should be careful not to confuse the concrete thing with the analytic "system." A "system" is an aspect of things in some degree abstracted from reality for purposes of analysis; the circulatory system of a mammal or the personality system of a human being are examples.

(2) In order to determine what lies within a particular system and what lies outside it, we need to specify the *boundaries* of that system. Sometimes this task is fairly easy, as in the case of the solar system or the United States Supreme Court, but often it requires an arbitrary decision. For example, what would we consider to be the boundaries of our two major parties? Would we include only party officials? Or would we also include all those who register as Democrats or Republicans? Or those who identify themselves as one or the other, even though they do not register? Or those who vote regularly for the one party or the other? Later on, I shall offer one definition of the "boundaries" of a political system.

(3) One system can be an element, a subsystem, of another. The earth is a subsystem of our solar system, which is a subsystem of our galaxy, which is a subsystem of the universe. The Foreign Relations Committee is a subsystem of the United States Senate, which is a subsystem of the Congress, and so on.

(4) Something may be a subsystem of two or more different systems that overlap only in part. A college professor might be an active member of the American Association of University Professors, the Democratic party, and the PTA.

It is useful to keep these observations in mind in considering the difference between a political system and a social system.

Political Systems and Social Systems

What is a democratic society? a free society? a socialist society? an authoritarian society? an international society? In what way is a social system distinguished from a political system?

Questions like these are particularly difficult to answer because the terms "society" and "social system" are used loosely, even by social scientists. In general, however, the term "social" is intended to be inclusive; economic and political relations are specific kinds of social relations. Although "social system" is sometimes given a more specific meaning, it too is a broad concept. Thus, Talcott Parsons, a leading American sociologist, defines a social system by three characteristics: (1) two or more persons interact; (2) in their actions they take account of how the others

Figure 2

are likely to act; and (3) sometimes they act together in pursuit of common goals.[8] A social system, then, is a very inclusive kind of order.

According to Parsons' usage, a political system or an economic system would be parts, aspects, or subsystems of a social system. This way of looking at the matter is illustrated in Figure 2, where AC represents the set of all political subsystems and ABC represents subsystems that can be considered as either political or economic, depending on which aspect we are concerned with. Examples of ABC would be General Motors, the United States Bureau of the Budget, or the Board of Governors of the Federal Reserve system.

Thus, a democratic *society* could be defined as a social system that has not only democratic political (sub)systems but also a number of other subsystems that operate to contribute directly or indirectly to the strength of the democratic political processes. Conversely, by definition, an authoritarian society would contain many important subsystems, such

[8]Talcott Parsons and Edward A. Shils, eds., *Toward a General Theory of Action* (Cambridge, Mass.: Harvard University Press, 1951), p. 55. For a discussion of the meaning and history of the concept "society," see *International Encyclopedia of the Social Sciences*, s.v. "society."

as the family, the churches, and the schools, all acting to strengthen authoritarian political processes. Let us consider two examples.

In his famous *Democracy in America* (1835–1840) the illustrious French writer Alexis de Tocqueville listed a number of "principal causes which tend to maintain the democratic republic in the United States." His list included not only the constitutional structure but also the absence of a large military establishment, equality in social and economic conditions, a prosperous agricultural economy, and the mores, customs, and religious beliefs of Americans.[9] In Tocqueville's view the prospects for a healthy democratic *political* system in the United States were strengthened enormously by the fact that a highly democratic Constitution was reinforced by many other aspects of the *society*. Hence American society could be called a democratic society.

By contrast, many observers were pessimistic about the prospects of democracy in Germany after World War II, because they believed that many aspects of German society were highly authoritarian and tended to undermine democratic political relations. They were mainly concerned with the wide tendency for social institutions of all kinds to take on a strong pattern of dominance and submission—the family, schools, churches, business, and all relations between government officials, whether policemen or civil servants, and ordinary citizens. The fact that political democracy had to be instituted in a predominantly authoritarian social environment was not particularly auspicious for the future of democracy in Germany. A number of recent observers, on the other hand, feel more optimistic about the future of political democracy in Germany precisely because they see evidence that the authoritarian character of other social institutions has been declining.

Government and State

In every society, people tend to develop more or less standard expectations about social behavior in various situations. One learns how to behave as a host or a guest, a parent or grandparent, a "good loser," a soldier, a bank clerk, a prosecutor, a judge, and so on. Patterns like these, in which a number of people share roughly similar expectations about behavior in particular situations, are called *roles*. We all play various roles and frequently shift from one role to another rapidly.

Whenever a political system is complex and stable, political roles develop. Perhaps the most obvious political roles are played by persons who create, interpret, and enforce rules that are binding on members of the political system. These roles are *offices*, and the collection of offices

---

[9]Alexis de Tocqueville, *Democracy in America*, vol. 1 (New York: Vintage Books, 1955), pp. 298–342.

in a political system constitutes the government of that system. At any given moment, of course, these offices, or roles, are (aside from vacancies) filled by particular individuals, concrete persons—Senator Foghorn, Judge Cranky, Mayor Twimbly. But in many systems the roles remain much the same even when they are played by a succession of individuals. To be sure, different actors may—and usually do—interpret the role of Hamlet or Othello in different ways, sometimes in radically different ways. So, too, with political roles. Jefferson, Jackson, Lincoln, Theodore Roosevelt, Wilson, and Franklin Roosevelt, for example, each enlarged the role of President beyond what he had inherited from his predecessors by building new expectations in people's minds about what a President should or legitimately could do in office. "There are as many different ways of being President," Nelson Polsby asserts, "as there are men willing to fill the office."[10] Yet expectations as to the proper role of the President also limit the extent to which he can make it what he wishes— a fact dramatized by President Johnson's decision in 1968 not to seek reelection because, in effect, he could no longer play the presidential role in the way that he believed the office required.

But—a reader might ask—in defining "government" as we have just done, don't we create a new problem for ourselves? If there is a great variety of political systems—from trade unions and universities to countries and international organizations—what about *the* Government? After all, the United States, as in most other countries, when you speak of *the* Government everyone seems to know what you mean. Of all the governments in the various associations of a particular territory, generally one is in some way recognized as *the* Government. How does the Government differ from other governments? Consider three possible answers:

(1) *The* Government pursues "higher" and "nobler" purposes than other governments. There are at least three difficulties with this proposal. First, because people disagree about what the "higher" or "nobler" purposes are, and even whether a given purpose is or is not being pursued at any given moment, this criterion might not be very helpful in trying to decide whether this or that government is *the* Government. Second, despite the fact that people often disagree over how to rank purposes or values and may even hold that *the* Government is pursuing evil ends, they still agree on what is and what is not *the* Government. An anarchist does not doubt that he is being oppressed by *the* Government.

[10]See Polsby's *Congress and the Presidency*, a companion book in this series. Polsby compares the presidents from Franklin Roosevelt to Gerald Ford. See also James David Barber, *The Presidential Character: Predicting Performance in the White House* (Englewood Cliffs, N.J.: Prentice-Hall, Inc., 1972).

Third, what about bad Governments? For example, do democratic and totalitarian Governments *both* pursue noble purposes? That point seems logically absurd.

Our first proposed answer, then, confuses the problem of defining Government with the more difficult and more important task of deciding on the criteria for a "good" or "just" Government. Before anyone can decide what the *best* Government is, he must know first what the Government is.

(2) Aristotle suggested another possibility: *the* Government is distinguished by the character of the association to which it pertains— namely, a political association that is self-sufficient, in the sense that it possesses all the qualities and resources necessary for a good life. This definition suffers from some of the same difficulties as the first. Moreover, if it were strictly applied, we should have to conclude that no Governments exist! Aristotle's idealized interpretation of the city-state was very far from reality even in his day. Athens was not self-sufficient culturally, economically, or militarily. In fact, she was quite unable to guarantee her own peace or independence; without allies, she could not even maintain the freedom of her own citizens. What was true of the Greek city-states is of course equally true today.

(3) *The* Government is *any government that successfully upholds a claim to the exclusive regulation of the legitimate use of physical force in enforcing its rules within a given territorial area.*[11] The political system made up of the residents of that territorial area and the Government of the area is a "State."[12]

This definition immediately suggests three questions:

(1) Can't individuals who aren't Government officials ever legitimately use force? What about parents who spank their children? The answer is, of course, that the Government of a State does not necessarily *monopolize* the use of force, but it has the exclusive authority to set the limits within which force may legitimately be used. The Governments of most States permit private individuals to use force in some circumstances. For example, although many Governments forbid cruel or excessive punishment of children, most permit parents to spank their own offspring. Boxing is permitted in many countries.

(2) What about criminals who go uncaught? After all, no country is free of assault, murder, rape, and other forms of violence, and criminals sometimes escape the law. The point is, however, that the claim of the

---

[11]Adapted from Weber, *Theory of Social and Economic Organization,* p. 154, by substituting "exclusive regulation" for "monopoly" and "rules" for "its order."

[12]Capitalized here to avoid confusion with constituent states in federal systems.

Government of the State to regulate violence and force is successfully upheld, in the sense that few people would seriously contest the exclusive right of the State to punish criminals. Although criminal violence exists, it is not legitimate.

(3) What about circumstances of truly widespread violence and force, such as civil war or revolution? In this case no single answer will suffice. (Remember the disadvantages of dichotomous definitions.) For brief periods, no State may exist at all, since no government is capable of upholding its claim to the exclusive regulation of the legitimate use of physical force. Several governments may contest for the privilege over the same territory. Or what was formerly a territory ruled by the Government of one State may now be divided and ruled by the Governments of two or more States, with gray stateless areas where they meet.

We can be reasonably sure of one thing: When large numbers of people in a particular territory begin to doubt or deny the claim of the Government to regulate force, then the existing State is in peril of dissolution.

WHAT IS POLITICAL ANALYSIS?

Whether a person likes it or not, virtually no one is completely beyond the reach of some kind of political system. A citizen encounters politics in the government of a country, town, school, church, business firm, trade union, club, political party, civic association, and a host of other organizations. Politics is an unavoidable fact of human existence. Everyone is involved in some fashion at some time in some kind of political system.

If politics is inescapable, so are the consequences of politics. That statement might once have been shrugged off as rhetorical, but today it is a brutal and palpable fact. For whether humankind is blown to smithereens or whether political arrangements that enable our species to survive will be reached is now being determined—by politics and politicians.

The answer to the question "Why analyze politics?" is, then, obvious. Some people may wish to study politics in a purely detached and contemplative way, but surely there are fields more rewarding for pure contemplation. The best reason for improving one's skill in political analysis is this: political analysis helps one to understand the world one lives in, to make more intelligent choices among the alternatives one faces, and to influence the changes inherent in all political systems. To act intelligently in politics requires that one carefully choose goals and achieve as many of them as possible at the minimum expense.

FOUR ORIENTATIONS

To understand and to act intelligently, we often ask a basic question that will of course vary from one situation to another. The question frequently goes something like this: How can I act in order to arrive at a better state of affairs (for me, my family, my business, my party, my country, the weak and suffering, the strong and able, the people, all of humanity, and so on)? But another question must be asked to answer the first: What would a better state of affairs be? More generally, what distinguishes the better from the worse? However, still a third question must be asked: How do things come about in the real world? For instance, if I believe that peace is better than war, and if I wish to prevent wars, I must therefore do something about the causes of wars. But what *are* the causes of wars? All three questions presuppose answers to a fourth, a question so fundamental that one often takes the answer for granted and is quite unaware that there *is* such a question: What do I *mean* by the key terms I use or the statements I make? For example, how do I define a *war*? How do I distinguish it from other forms of violence?

Each question represents a different orientation toward the world. In asking the first question, one is oriented to discovering a *policy*. In asking the second, one seeks to discover *norms*, or criteria, to judge alternative policies. In asking the third question, one seeks to discover *empirical* relationships among elements in the real world. In asking the fourth, one tries to clarify *meaning*. Hence we can speak of a policy orientation, a normative orientation, an empirical orientation, and a semantic orientation. Depending on which question is the focus of attention at any given moment in political analysis, one can speak of policy analysis, normative analysis, empirical analysis, and semantic analysis (sometimes referred to as conceptual analysis).

Empirical Orientation

Empirical analysis is most evident in the natural sciences, but it is also present in all the social and behavioral sciences.

Scientists seek systematically to describe, explain, and predict events within their domain of inquiry. They try to discover and describe statistical, probabilistic, functional, and causal relationships among events, things, and persons. Examples of apparently true empirical propositions are Galileo's inertial law, which states that if left to itself a body will move with uniform velocity in one direction; Newton's second law, that force equals mass times acceleration; Einstein's equation $e = mc^2$; and Boyle's law of gases. So are these less elegant but important and probably true propositions: that aspirin relieves pain, smoking causes lung cancer, and workers are more likely than middle-class persons to vote for leftist parties.

The empirical orientation, however, is not limited to science. Science is simply a more systematic and refined development of an orientation basic in each person. None of us could carry on daily life without an empirical orientation toward the world. Every action one takes—even if it is as simple as brushing one's teeth—is inescapably related to beliefs about the empirical nature of the world. These beliefs may, and often do, prove false. What is true for our beliefs in daily life is also true of scientific beliefs. In general, the validity of empirical propositions—even the "laws of science"—depends on how man perceives and interprets the world. Therefore, empirical propositions may be altered or refuted in the light of new observations, perceptions, experiments, or interpretations. It is important to remember, then, that when we speak of an empirical orientation, we have in mind a kind of implicit question; the explicit answer (belief, proposition, scientific law, or commonsense empirical assumption) may be wrong. "President Nixon was removed from office by a conviction on a vote of impeachment" is an empirical statement. It happens to be false.

Normative Orientation

Normative analysis is characteristic of religion and philosophy and is particularly evident in subjects such as ethics and political philosophy. Like the empirical orientation, the normative orientation is an inescapable part of our actions and beliefs. Even in the most mundane aspects of life we act on the belief that some things are better than others. Even one who professed to seek only self-interest would have *some* notions about the nature of his self-interest. Is it happiness? Money? Power? Self-indulgence?

When a normative orientation stimulates a more systematic pursuit of knowledge, it often seeks answers to questions such as: What do we mean by "good" and "better"? Is there a single best criterion for judging the good, such as happiness, freedom, equality, or justice? If not, how are these various goods related? On what grounds do we justify one or more of these criteria of goodness? How can we know what is good? Is our knowledge of what is good "objective" in roughly the same sense that knowledge in the natural sciences is thought to be "objective," or is it much more, perhaps totally, "subjective"? Are we obliged to seek the good? Why?

Policy Orientation

Policy analysis searches for policies or actions to close some of the gap between an existing state of affairs and a possible future that would be better. One sees that something is unsatisfactory, wants to arrive at a more satisfactory state of affairs, and looks for a solution: a policy that will take one from where one is to where one wants to be. Each of us engages in this kind of search whether choosing clothes, courses, colleges, or candidates.

In these times, systematic policy analysis is carried on by policy-makers and their staffs in government, business firms, banks, and innumerable other organizations. However, although the concrete practice of policy analysis must be as old as human thought, as a systematic intellectual activity it is comparatively new. In this respect, policy analysis differs from empirical and normative analysis, which have been systematic intellectual activities for several thousand years.

The essence of the policy orientation is a consideration of alternatives and their consequences. The desirability of adopting a policy depends on both the goals in view (for example, reducing unemployment) and the nature of the specific situation. (Is the economy undergoing inflation? stagnation? recession?) In practice, therefore, analysis of policy in a systematic way often reflects the special features of a concrete situation, the particular goals, and an empirical analysis drawn from some specialized domain of knowledge such as economics, political science, medicine, and so on. Whether policy analysis can develop into a specialized field of knowledge is a question which for the present seems to have no satisfactory answer.

Semantic Orientation

A *semantic analysis* tries to clarify meaning, particularly the meaning of key concepts (therefore it is sometimes referred to as conceptual analysis). The first chapter of this book, which tries to clarify the meaning of the term "politics," and this chapter, in which we attempt to understand "policy analysis," are both examples of semantic analysis. In the next chapter, when we explore the meaning of such key terms as power, influence, and authority, we shall also be engaged in the analysis of meaning.

Clarification of meaning is an important element of political analysis because many of the key concepts used in political analysis have no commonly accepted definition. Democracy, freedom, revolution, coercion, power, and equality, for example, are notoriously ambiguous terms. Their meanings vary even among professional political scientists and political philosophers. Attempts to clarify these different meanings, or to specify a particular meaning, have not resulted in general agreement.[1]

---

[1]Brief definitions of many political terms will be found in Edward C. Smith and Arnold J. Zurcher, *Dictionary of American Politics*, 2nd ed. (New York: Barnes & Noble, 1968). More extended efforts at clarifying meanings of many concepts used in the social sciences will be found in *International Encyclopedia of the Social Sciences*. The encyclopedia contains extended definitions of terms and a great deal of empirical analysis as well. See also Harold D. Lasswell and Abraham Kaplan, *Power and Society* (New Haven: Yale University Press, 1950).

HOW THE FOUR ORIENTATIONS ARE RELATED

It is sometimes said that empirical analysis seeks to provide knowledge of what is; the normative orientation, knowledge of what ought to be; and the policy orientation knowledge of how to proceed from what is to what ought to be. This is probably as accurate as any succinct statement can be. However, it would be a mistake to think that each orientation seeks knowledge of a kind that is completely independent of the others.

Policy analysis requires an understanding of both what is and what ought to be. Policy analysis is a specific combination applied to concrete circumstances of both empirical analysis and normative assumptions. A policy would be judged to be bad if it were based on a false understanding of the world so that it would not lead to the intended results. An example would be choosing a policy that is intended to halt inflation but which in fact has no effect or even worsens it. We would also judge a policy bad if it led to what we considered a bad consequence, even if these consequences were intended. The Nazi policy of exterminating Jews was bad because the goal itself was evil; the efficient means of extermination used by the Nazis only made the policy all the worse.

While it is rather obvious that in analyzing policy we must deal with both ends and means, it is sometimes supposed that normative analysis deals only with ends and empirical analysis only with means. The difficulty with this view, as I have already implied, is that all normative analysis presupposes some empirical belief. A presupposition may be some comparatively trivial, obvious, or generally accepted belief such as the belief that most people prefer pleasure to pain. However, any extended normative analysis usually rests on an elaborate set of empirical beliefs, the validity of which is not obvious or universally acknowledged.

It might seem reasonable to conclude, then, that policy analysis requires both the other kinds of analysis; that normative analysis requires empirical beliefs of some kind; but that empirical analysis can proceed without either normative or policy assumptions. In this perspective, science, including social science, tries to discover objective knowledge that is quite independent of norms of goodness or badness. The scientist seeks to discover and describe what is, not to prescribe what ought to be.

This view, however, raises a number of questions the answers to which are furiously debated: Is objective knowledge possible even in the natural sciences? If so, is it also possible in sciences having to do with human beings (the social and behavioral sciences)? Even if it should prove possible in the human sciences, would it be desirable to seek empirical knowledge with no concern for values?—These are all highly controversial questions.

Some writers argue that political analysis always involves, at least implicitly, empirical and normative orientations of some kind. Those who support this view can readily point to the fact that whether or not empirical political analysis theoretically could be carried on independently of normative and policy orientations, in practice empirical, normative, and policy orentations often are mingled together in political analysis. Indeed, sometimes these orientations become so entangled that one cannot be certain of the author's intentions. If we were to read that "Americans have always preferred democracy to other forms of government," we might wonder whether the author intends this statement to be interpreted purely as an empirical description, or whether he recommends democracy to his readers as the best form of government. Clearly the meaning we give to propositions of this kind depends partly on what we believe the author's intention was. To the extent that we misinterpret intentions, we also misinterpret the meaning of speech or writing. This kind of ambiguity is common in political analysis, not only because the political analyst fails to make his intentions clear but also because the reader or listener often imputes an orientation that may not have been intended.[2]

SEMANTIC ANALYSIS:
THE PROBLEM OF DEFINITIONS

Policy analysis, normative analysis, and empirical analysis all require certain assumptions that rarely are made explicit in the analysis itself. For example, all empirical analysis depends on the assumption that the universe is not utterly random or chaotic, that it has certain regularities, that some of these regularities can be detected, that evidence for the existence of a regularity in the past furnishes a rational ground for expecting the same regularity under the same circumstances in the future, and so on. Behind every explorable assumption there usually lies still another explorable assumption. To avoid what might be called an infinite regress of inquiry, every kind of analysis starts with some assumptions that are taken as given.

In addition to various philosophical assumptions, all three kinds of political analysis presuppose a considerable amount of agreement on the meaning of elemental terms. Some terms simply have to be left undefined, otherwise we should be engaged forever in an infinite regression of definition, in which each term is defined by using other terms, which in turn have to be defined by using still other terms, *ad infinitum*. For most

---

[2]Almost everyone who writes about politics must have had this experience. I have been astounded at how often my intended descriptive statements are interpreted as my own normative judgments.

terms we stop, more or less arbitrarily, with meanings we believe are contained in ordinary language.

One source of difficulty, however, is that some people (including scholars) may disagree not only about terms but also as to what a definition of a term is supposed to do. Although not always greeted with enthusiasm, one common way to clarify the meaning of a key term is for a speaker or writer simply to stipulate the definition he is using, presumably one that is consistent with important meanings found in ordinary language and recorded in dictionaries. A definition stipulated in this way is sometimes called a *nominal* definition of a term. A nominal definition is a proposed treaty, so to speak, governing the use of terms.[3]

To be clearheaded about terms often helps one to be clearheaded about politics, an activity in which language is ambiguous and often used for propagandistic purposes. Yet one ought to realize, too, the limitations of definitions. Norminal definitions do not reveal anything about "fact," about what goes on in the "real" world. Nothing can be proved true or false about the real political world (or economy or whatever) by only defining a term. Definitions may help us to understand our language, but they do not, unaided, help us to understand what the "real" world is like. For that we need *empirical propositions,* which assert more than a definition, something that can, if only in principle, be confirmed or refuted by experience.

Here, for example, is an empirical statement: In 1974, no country with a per capita GNP of less than $200 a year had a legal opposition party with more than 10 percent of the seats in Parliament. To decide if this statement is true, we must have some of the terms carefully defined. What, for example, is meant by "a legal opposition party?" But no matter how long definitions are discussed, finally we shall not be able to prove the validity of the proposition unless we examine some "facts"—empirical data, evidence, experience, and information about the "real" world, call it what you will. (Incidentally, the proposition is falsified by at least one case: India.) Once made, this point must seem obvious, yet the failure to distinguish between a definition and an empirical proposition is common in political analysis.

Consider, for example, the much-debated question of the relationships between capitalism, socialism, and democracy. Using terms defined

[3]There is a voluminous literature on definitions and their place in the empirical sciences. To explore further, the reader could start with Felix E. Oppenheim, "The Language of Political Inquiry: Problems of Clarification," in *The Handbook of Political Science,* vol 1, ed. Fred I. Greenstein and Nelson W. Polsby (Reading, Mass.: Addison-Wesley Publishing Co., 1975). See also the judicious discussion in Abraham Kaplan, *The Conduct of Inquiry* (San Francisco: Chandler Publishing Co., 1964), Chapter Two, and Vernon Van Dyke, *Political Science: A Philosophical Analysis* (Stanford, Calif.: Stanford University Press, 1960), Chapter Six.

	The political system is:	The economic system is:
I	A Democracy	Capitalism
II	A Democracy	Socialism
III	A Dictatorship	Capitalism
IV	A Dictatorship	Socialism

Figure 3

in Chapter One, we could list four relationships that are logically possible (see Figure 3). None of these combinations is excluded by definition. Whether each combination actually does exist, or how likely it may be, are questions that would require some empirical analysis of past and present political and economic systems. Is it true, as advocates of capitalism sometimes argue, that democracy could not exist in industrial nations without a capitalist economy? Is it true, as Lenin and other communists have argued, that a capitalist economy can exist only under a political dictatorship? Although questions like these are not easy to answer, we could never answer them simply by debating definitions. The important point is that stipulating definitions may help in semantic analysis, which in turn may help us to understand the meaning of statements contained in policy analysis, normative analysis, and empirical analysis. But semantic analysis can never substitute for policy analysis, normative analysis, or empirical analysis.

POLITICAL ANALYSIS AND POLITICAL SCIENCE

In the fields of teaching and research in American colleges and universities, the term *political science* (rather than political analysis) has come to be widely used in this century, initially in the United States, but increasingly since the mid-century in the rest of the world as well.[4] The subject matter of political science departments and of political science scholars is, of course, political analysis.

[4]In some countries, such as France and Italy, the term political science has been used to cover a number of specialized fields such as law, economics, and sociology. In these countries, political analysis was until recently assumed to be an aspect of each of these fields, but not an autonomous intellectual discipline. Consequently, among the "political sciences" there was no separate field of political science.

Although the name "political science" suggests an exclusive orientation toward empirical analysis, this is not the case.[5] Political scientists and academic departments of political science are concerned with all four kinds of political analysis. Although political science departments offer courses intended to provide a description and understanding of political systems—what is rather than what ought to be—they have also offered courses that stress normative ideas, particularly as developed by the great political philosophers. Like the philosophers themselves, many courses combine normative and empirical analysis. Indeed, probably few political science courses are confined strictly to empirical analysis; and as we have seen already, any course that concentrates on normative analysis must include empirical analysis as well. Thus Aristotle's *Politics* contains a vital discussion on the subject of revolutions. And because no course in political science is likely to proceed for long without some attention to concepts, semantic analysis is always included.

A good bit of political science has always contained implicit analysis of policy. Like others who are deeply interested in political life, most political scientists naturally have strong personal views on matters of public policy. However, only recently have many political scientists sought to develop intellectual tools useful in understanding the policy alternatives available in a particular situation and arriving at a recommended policy.[6] It is still too early to assert what the specific contribution from political scientists to policy analysis will be.[7] It may be that as academic subject matter, policy analysis must cut across the "policy sciences," such as political science, law, and economics.

EMPIRICAL POLITICAL ANALYSIS: ART OR SCIENCE?

Is empirical political analysis a science? Or is it an art? I believe it is both. To the extent that many aspects of political analysis are most easily acquired by practice and training under the supervision of a person already skilled in this area, it is an art. Whenever students of politics

[5]American scholars who helped inaugurate the first departments of political science in this country were strongly influenced by scholarship in nineteenth-century Germany, where the term *wissenschaft* connoted not only science but also learning, knowledge, scholarship, and more generally, the intellectual product of any systematic inquiry. Thus the word "science" in "political science" was probably intended to mean something like "systematic study" and not, as it is more likely to be interpreted today, "empirical inquiry in the manner of the natural sciences." For a brief history, see Dwight Waldo, "Political Science: Tradition, Discipline, Profession, Science, Enterprise," in *The Handbook of Political Science*, vol. 1.

[6]As late as 1951, none of the chapters in *The Policy Sciences*, ed. Daniel Lerner and Harold D. Lasswell (Stanford, Calif.: Stanford University Press, 1951) specifically discussed the tasks of political analysis, although both editors were political scientists.

[7]References to recent works on policy-making will be found in the appendix.

scrupulously test their generalizations and theories against the data of experience by means of meticulous observation, classification, and measurement, then empirical political analysis is scientific in its approach. To the extent that this approach actually yields tested propositions of considerable generality, political analysis can be regarded as scientific in its results.

The extent to which empirical political analysis should be approached as an art or a science is a hotly debated issue. And if it is considered a science, there are important differences between those who seeks to emulate the natural sciences like physics and chemistry, and those who believe that the study of human beings is inherently different from the study of nature in its nonhuman manifestations.

Many who hold the second view argue that we cannot really understand a human action unless we can grasp its subjective meaning: what it means to the person who performs it, what that person intended by it, and so on. An atomic particle does not intend anything; what it does has no subjective meaning to the physicist. Physics does well as a science by describing activity in purely external, physical terms. But even so simple an action as voting cannot be understood as merely a physical activity. We could imagine how voting might be perceived by an invisible observer from Mars who knew no human language and hadn't the faintest idea what those peculiar earthmen were doing when they entered an enclosed booth and pulled a little lever or scratched some black marks on a piece of paper. For all the Martian knows, a person who votes and a person who makes a call from a telephone booth are both performing similar acts.

The incompleteness of purely external, physical descriptions of human activity, combined with the difficulty of arriving at an adequate understanding of the subjective features that give human action so much of its meaning, have led some scholars to the pessimistic view that a "scientific" understanding of human action is impossible. Others optimistically view the problems posed as difficult but not insuperable. The pessimistic view suffers from the usual weakness of perfectionism. In this case, the perfectionist appears to be saying that there is nothing worthwhile between utter ignorance, at one extreme, and knowledge of regularities as exhibited in the laws of physics and chemistry, at the other. This is absurd. Some reduction in our uncertainty is better than total uncertainty. No one seriously argues that systematic inquiry can never improve our knowledge, thus reducing our uncertainty.

It is true, however, that uncertainty appears to be a prime characteristic of all political life. Systematic political analysis can reduce some of that uncertainty. Yet even the best political analysis leaves a large element of uncertainty in our understanding of political life. For the foreseeable future, perhaps the only certainty about political life will be its uncertainty. Hence, intelligent political action will have to be based on the assumption that political knowledge has distinct limits, even though these are not permanent. In following chapters, we shall encounter a number of the factors that create uncertainties in our political knowledge. In Chapter Ten, I shall suggest ways of coping with uncertainty in developing policies.

POLITICAL ANALYSIS AND POLITICAL PRACTICE

Even though they overlap, we must not mistake systematic political analysis with political practice. Like critics in the arts, a person able to analyze is not necessarily a gifted performer.

Skill in analyzing politics is not the same as skill in practicing politics. James Madison's speeches at the Constitutional Convention and his chapters in *The Federalist* demonstrate that he was a brilliant political analyst, yet he was a mediocre President. By contrast, Franklin Roosevelt had enormous skill, insight, and astuteness as a political leader and President; yet one cannot find in Roosevelt's messages, state papers, and letters an analysis of how he himself operated as President that seems as valid as the analysis contained in several later studies by scholars. Even if Roosevelt had tried to explain how he operated, could he have succeeded? The skilled artist is frequently unable to explain why or how he does what he does so superbly.

Sometimes, to be sure, skill in political practice does go hand-in-hand with skill in political analysis. Woodrow Wilson was a historian and political scientist before he was a politician. *Congressional Government,* which he wrote in 1884 at the age of twenty-eight, is still widely read, nearly a century later. As governor of New Jersey and as President, Wilson also displayed a high order of skill as a political practitioner—until opposition to his goals during his second term brought out aspects of his personality that severely impaired his skills as a politician.[8] Moreover, every skilled political practitioner must have some capacity for political analysis, even though he may be unable to explain what he knows. The rapidly increasing complexity of modern national and international politics requires a corresponding increase in the analytical competence of political leaders. The old-fashioned ward-heeler whose

---

[8]In his analysis of Wilson's personality and political conduct, Alexander L. George shows that when Wilson met genuinely threatening opposition, as he did during his second term, he "was unable to function expediently and proved singularly gauche as a politician. . . . Wilson became rigidly stubborn and tried to force through his proposal without compromising it." See "Power as a Compensatory Value for Political Leaders," *Journal of Social Issues* 24 (July 1968): 42. See also Alexander L. George and Juliette L. George, *Woodrow Wilson and Colonel House: A Personality Study* (New York: Dover Press, 1964).

political knowledge was narrow and parochial is disappearing from American politics, in part because he cuts such a sorry figure against the backdrop of the complex problems of an age of nuclear energy and man-made satellites.

SOME UNAVOIDABLE POLITICAL QUESTIONS

Politics is an ancient and universal experience. In particular, political analysis has thrived in all cultures that have inherited the enormous legacy of that ancient people, few in number yet great in influence, the Greeks of the pre-Christian era. Like many other arts and sciences, political analysis achieved an extraordinary degree of sophistication among the Greeks twenty-five centuries ago under the tutelage of Socrates, Plato, and Aristotle. Since then, every age in Western civilization has furnished history with a few great students of politics who have tried to answer fundamental questions. In fact, it is no great exaggeration to say that all great political theorists whose works are of contemporary interest have asked similar political questions. Among the most important of these general questions are the following:

(1) What is the role of power and influence in political systems? (See Chapters Three and Four.) For example: Is there a "ruling elite" in the United States? an "Establishment"? a "power structure"? a "white power structure"?

(2) What do political systems have in common and in what ways do they differ from one another? (See Chapters Five and Six.) For example: Is political inequality an inescapable element in all political systems?

(3) What conditions induce stability, change, or revolution in different political systems? What is required if peace is to be maintained and violence avoided? What are the prerequisites for a stable democracy? (See Chapter Seven.) For example: How, if at all, can popular governments succeed in the emerging nations? Would rapid economic development help popular governments to prevent military overthrows in these countries?

(4) How do men behave in politics? What are the distinguishing features of *Homo politicus?* (See Chapter Eight.) For example: Are politicians mainly power-seekers?

(5) What sort of political system is the best? How can we evaluate different political systems? (See Chapter Nine.) For example: Can Americans justify the belief that democracy is the best political system?

(6) How can we act wisely in the midst of the great uncertainty that appears to be characteristic of political life? (See Chapter Ten.) For

example: Should governments engage in more experimentation before arriving at decisions about policies?

The first question requires an analysis of meaning, in the course of which a definition of the key term must be stipulated. The next three questions involve mainly empirical analysis. The fifth requires more discussion of normative analysis, and the last more discussion of policy analysis.

All the questions are endowed with the childlike simplicity found in humanity's persistent questions of life. They are easy to pose, enormously difficult to answer. This book does not furnish the answers. Instead, it provides a few of the analytical tools needed to search for the answers in an intelligent way.

POLITICAL
INFLUENCE

"Control," "power," "influence," and "authority" are words not exclusive to political practitioners and political theorists. One hears of the power to govern, the power of the purse, spiritual power, economic power, national power, presidential power, and Black Power.

Thus we all speak of power and assume that others know what we mean. The concept of power, as we saw in Chapter One, is central to political analysis; the notion of politics and a political system presupposes that words like control, power, authority, and influence have a definite meaning. The fact is, however, that these words are ambiguous; their meaning is elusive and complex.

THE ABSENCE OF STANDARD TERMINOLOGY

With words like power and influence neither in ordinary language nor in political science is there agreement on terms and definitions. Like others, political scientists use a variety of terms: power, influence, authority, control, persuasion, might, force, coercion. Let us, for convenience, simply call these "influence-terms." Like others, political scientists frequently do not define these terms; and when they do, they do not agree with each other. Although influence-terms have been central to political analysis throughout history, most theorists seem to have assumed, as did Aristotle, that they needed no great elaboration, presumably because their meaning would be understood by men of common sense.[1] Even Machiavelli, who was fascinated by the play of power, used a variety of undefined terms to describe and explain political life. In fact, the last several decades probably have witnessed more systematic efforts to tie down these concepts than have the previous millennia of political thought.[2] As a result, there has been a vast improvement in the clarity of the concepts. Yet it is still true that writers do not use influence-terms in the same way: one man's "influence" is another man's "power." For the time being, I shall use these terms as if they were interchangeable.

THREE FALLACIES IN THE ANALYSIS OF POWER

The Lump-of-Power Fallacy. Power is thought of often as if it were a single, solid, unbreakable lump. The lump can be passed from one actor to another, but cannot be shared. Either one has *the* power or one has *no* power. Presumably it is a similar notion that many people, in particular journalists, hold when they ask, "Who has the power around here?"

In contrast to wealth, income, social status, and other matters of value, many people do not conceive of power as a variable with a number of possible values. To them it has only two values: 0 or 1. Because wealth or income can take on many values—10 cents, $5.00, $35,000, $3 million, and so on—one can imagine different ways in which it might be distributed among the members of a group. When power is thought of as a lump, however, it can be distributed in only one way: some have all the power, and the rest have none.[3]

---

[1]An interesting attempt to clarify the meaning of various influence-terms by analyzing their usage in "ordinary" language (actually the language of highly educated writers) will be found in Hanna Pitkin, *Wittgenstein and Justice* (Berkeley: University of California, 1972), pp. 276 ff.

[2]References will be found on pp. 148–150.

[3]The lump-of-power fallacy occurs even in important works in social theory. A leading example is Ralf Dahrendorf's influential book *Class and Class Conflict in Industrial Society,* (Stanford, Calif.: Stanford University Press, 1956), pp. 166, 167, 171–173. See also the definitions 2.1, 2.1.1, and 2.1.2 on p. 237. Dahrendorf adds the following highly important qualification at p. 173, which, however, entirely drops out of his account: "This is not to say, of course, that there is no difference between those who have a great deal and those who have merely a little authority. Among the positions of domination there may be, and often is, considerable differentiation. But such differentiation, *while important for empirical analysis,* leaves unaffected the existence of a border line somewhere between those who have whatever little authority and the 'outs.' Strictly speaking, an analytical statement which states that there is a dichotomy of authority positions is tautological; but as this example shows, there are tautologies which are worth stating." [Emphasis added] One might add: tautologies may be worth stating but they are hardly worth presenting as the crucial assumption of an empirical theory. For another example, where the author explicitly follows Dahrendorf's lead, see I. Balbus, "The Concept of Interest in Pluralist and Marxist Analysis," *Politics and Society* 1 (February 1971):151–177.

An effort to treat wealth, income, or status in this dichotomous manner would impose an absurd and unnecessary handicap on our capacity to describe the way in which these are distributed, say, in the United States. Although the difficulties of measuring power are great, there is no reason why power, authority, control, or influence need to be conceived of in this fashion.

Confounding Power with Resources. Compare these two statements:

> Money is influence.
>
> In deciding to increase milk subsidies, the President was influenced by the milk producers, because they had contributed heavily to his campaign.

In the first statement, money and influence appear to be equivalent. Or perhaps money is conceived of as one kind of influence. Is the intention, then, to define influence? If so, wherever the term influence occurs, we could simply substitute the word money. Should we try to do so, however, we would quickly see that the substitution leads to confusion and even absurdity. Additionally, it would fail to catch the full meaning of what we wanted to say. Consider, for example,

> The President has a great deal of influence over Congress when it makes decisions as to the level of military spending.

Suppose we try to substitute "money" for "influence":

> The President has a great deal of money . . . over Congress? . . . in dealing with Congress? . . . for influencing Congress? . . .

Something has gone wrong. We don't quite know how to complete the sentence without either changing the meaning of "influence" or destroying the supposed equivalence of "money" and "influence."

When we simply define influence or power as equivalent to resources, we not only lose specificity as to subject matter but also we ignore an important empirical problem—whether and how the relation of influence is to be explained by the way in which one of the actors in the relationship uses resources. We simply deal with the problem of explanation by fiat: we assert a relationship, but we do not investigate it, let alone try to demonstrate it.

Confounding Power With Rewards and Deprivations. Consider the following:

[a] Because they had contributed heavily to his campaign,
[b] the President was influenced by the milk producers,
[c] in deciding to increase milk subsidies. As a result,
[d] the incomes of the milk producers were increased.

Notice that [d] is a *consequence* of [c], the President's decision (and therefore indirectly a consequence of [a] and [b]). The President's decision helps to explain the increase in the incomes of the milk producers, just as [a] helps to explain [b] and [c]. These relationships are shown in Figure 4.

If we were to define influence or power as exactly equivalent to its consequences for the allocation of rewards and deprivations, we once again would deal with empirical questions by fiat. We would not demonstrate a relationship, we would proclaim it. It might be supposed that the existence of a difference between an influence-relationship [b] with respect to certain kinds of decisions or outcomes [c], and the consequences of that relationship for rewards and deprivations [d] is so obvious that no one would confound the two. Unfortunately that is not so. Important works in social theory do sometimes confound the two.[4]

Figure 4

[4] For example, see Frank Parkin, *Class Inequality and Political Order* (New York: Praeger, 1971), p. 46. Earlier Parkin seems to commit the lump-of-power fallacy (p. 26). Incidentally, while Dahrendorf is highly critical of Marx's theory of classes, Parkin is more sympathetic. It is interesting that the lump-of-power fallacy may be independent of ideology.

WHAT WE MEAN BY INFLUENCE

There is general agreement that influence-terms refer to relationships among human beings. I may speak of man's power over nature or my power over my dog; a theologian may speak of God's power, or divine influence on events. But in political analysis, influence terms are usually restricted to relationships among human actors.

For the moment, we can capture the meaning of one general type of human relationship that might be called *manifest* or *explicit* influence. Suppose you were to stand on a street corner and say to yourself, "I command all automobile drivers on this street to drive on the right-hand side of the road"; suppose also that all the drivers actually did as you "commanded" them to do. Most people would regard you as mentally ill if you were to insist that you had just shown enough influence over automobile drivers to compel them to use the right-hand side of the road. On the other hand, suppose a policeman is standing in the middle of an intersection at which most traffic ordinarily moves ahead; he orders all traffic to turn right or left; the traffic moves right or left as he orders it to do. Then common sense suggests that the policeman acting in this particular role influences automobile drivers to turn right or left rather than go ahead.

Our common sense notion, then, goes something like this: suppose there are only two people in a system, A and B. A influences B to the extent that he changes B's actions or predispositions in some way.

Power as Cause

To clarify the notion of influence by appealing to common sense understandings, I have used terms like "induce," "cause," and "bring about." Consequently, a number of writers have suggested that influence be defined as a special kind of causal relation: thus the expression "A influences B to do x" could be recast as "A causes B to do x."[5]

Yet suppose that Albert and Betty are walking along the sidewalk, Albert accidentally bumps Betty, and Betty drops her packages. It is certainly correct to say that Albert (unintentionally) *caused* Betty to drop her packages, but we would not ordinarily say that Albert *influenced* Betty

[5]Because Bertrand Russell and several other philosophers attempted several generations ago to dismiss causal explanation as unnecessary in science, some analysts have been timid about treating causation as civilly as I do here. However, Russell's attempt to banish causation from the vocabulary of science was unsuccessful. Whatever may be the case with the formal vocabulary of physics, the physicist cannot carry on his experiments and the rest of us cannot act upon the world without some concept of causation. For a philosophical treatment of cause germane to human action, see Georg Henrik von Wright, *Explanation and Understanding* (Ithaca, N.Y.: Cornell University Press, 1971).

to drop her packages. If Albert really wanted Betty to drop her packages, perhaps to embarrass her, or to steal her packages, or to play a joke, or to introduce himself—in any of these cases we should be inclined to say that Albert influenced Betty to drop her packages.

It appears, then, that when we single out influence from all the other aspects of a human interaction in order to give it special attention, what interests us and what we focus attention on is that one or more of the persons in this interaction get what they want, or at least get closer to what they want, by causing other people to act in some particular way. We want to call attention to a *causal relationship* between what A wants and what B does. Recently Nagel has proposed a formulation that specifically emphasizes these features, which, paraphrased, states:

> Influence is a relation among actors such that the wants, desires, preferences, or intentions of one or more actors affect the actions, or predispositions to act, of one or more other actors.[6]

Manifest and Implicit Influence

Nagel has shown that a definition of influence along these lines enables one to deal with a long standing difficulty more successfully than definitions that had been proposed previously: the problem of A's implicit influence over B arising from *anticipations* by B as to what A wants. The nature of implicit influence can be made clearer if we first distinguish it from manifest influence:

> If A wants outcome x; if A acts with the intention of causing B to bring about x; and if as a result of A's actions, B attempts to bring about x, then A exercises *manifest* influence over B.

Manifest influence is easier to detect than implicit influence arising from anticipations. The "rule of anticipated reactions" was introduced by

---

[6]Nagel's definition of power is: "A power relation, actual or potential, is an actual or potential causal relation between the preferences of an actor regarding an outcome and the outcome itself." Jack H. Nagel, *The Descriptive Analysis of Power* (New Haven: Yale University Press, 1975), p. 29. Nagel himself sees "no reason not to apply the definition . . . to power of human actors over nonsocial outcomes (e.g., the weather)" (fn. 16, p. 29). I believe, however, that in political analysis the definition will be more useful if it is restricted to "social outcomes," that is, to relationships involving human actors. In any case, that is how it is used in this book. Nagel's emphasis on the causal aspects of influence is not original, nor does he claim so. In 1953, Herbert A. Simon advanced this idea in his influential "Notes on the Observation and Measurement of Political Power," (*Journal of Politics* 15 [1953]: 500–516). In the same year C. E. Lindblom and I, using the term control where Simon used power, wrote: "In loose language, A controls the responses of B if A's acts cause B to respond in a definite way." (*Politics, Economics, and Welfare* [New York: Harper & Brothers, 1953], p. 94.) However, believing that the concept of causation was itself unclear, I usually preferred other language. Nagel's contribution is to show more fully and rigorously than previous writers the implications and uses of a causal conception of influence.

Friedrich in 1937[7] to refer to a situation in which "one actor, B, shapes his behavior to conform to what he believes are the desires of another actor, A, without having received explicit messages about A's wants or intentions from A or A's agents."[8]

Friedrich offered examples to show that if one were to concentrate attention exclusively on manifest influence, one would often underestimate or entirely miss the influence of an important actor, such as the influence of the British Parliament on the conduct of foreign affairs by the Foreign Office.[9] Without taking anticipations into account, one would find it difficult to explain the full effects of elections on elected officials. To the extent that an elected official is guided by the outcome of the preceding election, he is manifestly influenced by voters; to the extent that he is guided by his desire to be reelected and his expectations of future reactions of voters or campaign contributors to his present conduct, then he is subject to the implicit influence of voters and campaign contributors. Earlier definitions made it difficult to deal with the instances like these in which influence is mediated by anticipated reactions. Now, however, we can define implicit influence in a fashion consistent with the general definition of influence given on page 30:

> If A wants outcome x, then although A does not act with the intention of causing B to bring about x, if A's desire for x causes B to attempt to bring about x, then A exercises implicit influence over B.

Although formally it will do the job, the language of this definition is formidable. Another example may help. Until Wilbur Mills resigned his chairmanship shortly after his reelection in 1974 in the wake of a personal scandal, he was widely acknowledged to be one of the most influential members of the Congress because of his key role as Chairman of the House Committee on Ways and Means, which has jurisdiction over all tax legislation. That Mills was highly influential within his committee is hardly open to doubt. Nor can it be questioned that the decisions of the committee in turn had enormous influence on the prospects in the Congress for action on tax matters.[10] Yet it appears that the committee and the House also had considerable influence over Mills.

---

[7]Carl J. Friedrich, *Constitutional Government and Democracy* (New York: Harper & Brothers, 1937), pp. 16–18.

[8]Nagel, *Analysis of Power*, p. 16.

[9]Carl J. Friedrich, *Man and His Government* (New York: McGraw-Hill Book Co., 1963), pp. 201–202.

[10]"The Committee is widely thought (and expected) to be the master of its esoteric subject matter, and in exchange for this expertise the House voluntarily gives up its right to amend Ways and Means bills . . ." John F. Manley, *The Politics of Finance: The House Committee on Ways and Means* (Boston: Little, Brown & Co., 1970), p. 72.

As to the House, after one of the first major bills Mills took to the floor was voted down, he was always exceedingly cautious to avoid bringing out a bill that might be defeated. Thus, because of his effort to anticipate the reactions of the House, the members of that body exercised implicit influence over Mills. Moreover, within his committee he was a persistent and industrious seeker after consensus. The author of a study of the committee remarks: "The essence of a consensus-seeking form of leadership, the kind practiced by Mills, is mutual dependence, a relationship between Mills and the committee that involves the flow of influence from the committee to Mills just as much as the flow from Mills to the committee."[11] Thus, it would appear that the committee's influence on Mills was a mixture of both manifest and implicit influence.

WHAT WE MEAN BY MORE INFLUENCE

Now that we have seen why a causal definition along the lines just set out seems best suited to our purpose, we must confront a major problem: how to describe the relative influence of different actors in a political system, or of the same actor in different times or circumstances.

An analogy may help. Economists, census-takers, and policy-makers often want to know how income and wealth are distributed in a country. How great is income inequality in the United States? How much, if at all do taxes change the distribution of income? Is the gap in incomes between whites and blacks decreasing? Between men and women in the labor force?

In measuring income, one great advantage economists have is the existence of money as a medium of exchange. Although money provides a convenient unit for measuring income, it is not a perfect measure of everything that might constitute income. Nevertheless, for many purposes what we really want to know about is income received in the form of money: money income. But how would one go about measuring the relative amount of power or influence of different actors in a system? A satisfactory measure would enable us to determine different amounts of influence in somewhat the same way that test scores are used to determine IQ, degrees determine temperature, or money determines income. At a minimum, we could then decide whether Addy's influence was more than Bret's, Bret's more than Calvin's, (and thus Addy's more than Calvin's), and so on. Unfortunately, however, no one has yet been able to show how we might meaningfully describe the distribution of influence

[11]*Ibid.*, p. 122. See also pp. 105, 106, and 108.

in the same way that we can describe the distribution of IQ test scores among school children, or yesterday's noon temperature in various cities of the world, or the incomes of American families.[12]

Scope and Domain

The domain of an actor's influence consists of the other actors influenced by him. The scope of an actor's influence refers to the matters on which he can influence them. In exercising influence, then, an actor influences a domain of other actors with respect to a certain scope of their actions or predispositions.

We can add up a family's income from different sources—salary, rents, interest, dividends, and so on—to arrive at its total income. We can then add up the total incomes of some category of families—the poorest 25 percent, blacks, the elderly, wage earners—and arrive at an aggregate figure for that category. In the case of influence, however, it is difficult enough to estimate relative influence within a particular scope and domain; it is by no means clear how we can "add up" influence over many different scopes and domains in order to arrive at total, or aggregate, influence.

Any statement about influence that does not clearly indicate the domain and scope it refers to verges on being meaningless. When one hears that A is highly influential, the proper question is: Influential over what actors with respect to what matters? The failure to insist on this simple question often leads political observers astray. For example, several pioneering efforts that helped to trigger off a large number of studies of community power paid scant attention to the possibility that people who are regarded as leaders in a community might be influential on some matters but not others. As investigators became more concerned with differences in "scopes" of influence, they began to discover that a community leader's influence is often highly specialized: a person influences decisions about schools, let us say, but not about zoning; or a person is

---

[12]In the technical language of measurement theory, IQ scores provide an *ordinal* scale that allows us only to rank different persons according to their test scores. Degrees of temperature provide an *interval* scale as well, because the intervals between units are assumed to be equal. Therefore, not only can we rank the different cities from cooler to warmer, according to their noon temperatures, but we can also say that the difference between Portland, Maine, (70°) and Portland, Oregon, (60°) was the same as between Chicago (90°) and Washington (100°). Money provides a *ratio* scale because we can not only rank and compare differences but we can also compare ratios, i.e., Amy's annual income of $12,000 is twice as great as Bret's income of $6,000. Although a valid and reliable ordinal scale for comparing influence within a particular scope and domain seems to me the most we can hope for, discussions about power and influence often imply the existence of a higher level of measurement for total influence.

influential on urban redevelopment but not on political nominations or elections.[13]

Amount: Within a Given Scope and Domain

The problem of how to "add up" an actor's influence with respect to different scopes, let alone "add up" influence with respect to different scopes over different domains of persons, has proved intractable. If influence is a form of causation, then the amount of A's influence over an outcome should be equivalent to the amount of the outcome (B's actions) or predispositions caused by A's desires. As direct as this approach is, theorists have shied away from it because there are difficulties in measuring the amount of an effect attributable to a supposed cause. A definition along these lines, it appeared, would translate one definition into another, but it would still not offer a way of measuring influence.

Nagel argues, however, that the amount of power, so defined, can be measured by means of a statistical technique called path analysis.[14] Unfortunately, the theory of path analysis assumes a level of mathematical proficiency beyond that of many political analysts. Moreover, the application of path analysis requires a measurement level beyond what is ordinarily available in order to observe the exercise of influence.[15]

Despite these acute disadvantages, Nagel's proposal for measuring the relative amount of power of different actors has significant value for illuminating and guiding thought and research involving the concept of influence. It boils down to the essential question: How much do the wants or desires of some actors effect the actions or predispositions of others?

[13]Thus a political scientist who studied "The Elites of Atlanta" discovered that a group of fifty-seven persons who were reported by well-informed observers of the Atlanta scene to be influential in making important community decisions were rarely key actors on more than one of three key issues studied. The three issues were a bond program, a mayoralty election, and urban renewal. Of the fifty-seven with a reputation for influence, only twelve were key actors on two issues, and only four were key actors on all three issues. M. Kent Jennings, *Community Influentials: The Elites of Atlanta* (New York: Free Press, 1964), p. 160, Table 21. I have calculated the figures from percentages in the table.

[14]Nagel, *Analysis of Power*, pp. 55 ff. For a brief discussion of other measures see *ibid.*, Chapter Six, "Measures of Power," pp. 83–99. Nagel shows that a measure I proposed some years ago is a special case of his. See my article "The Concept of Power," *Behavioral Science* 2 (July 1957): 201–215. This has been reprinted together with many other articles on the subject in Roderick Bell, David V. Edwards, and R. Harrison Wagner, eds., *Political Power, A Reader in Theory and Research* (New York: Free Press, 1969).

[15]Nagel's demonstration of path analysis assumes variables measured on interval scales. (Cf. fn. 12, *supra*, p. 33.) "The appropriateness of path analysis for ordinal data remains a major unsettled issue.... The controversy is not one I can resolve, though the use of path analysis with ordinal data is obviously an appealing possibility. An answer is not crucial for the primarily heuristic applications of path analysis in this book.... Those who would apply path analysis in empirical power research, however, must take the level of measurement problem into account." *Ibid.*, p. 73.

No matter what techniques one may use to arrive at an answer, if power is conceived of as a kind of causation, then surely this is the right question to ask.

Total Amount of Influence

If one were to use this measure to estimate an actor's influence within a given scope and domain, one still would face the problem of adding an actor's influence in various scopes and domains to arrive at an aggregate. How could we determine, for example, whether the President is, in the aggregate, more powerful than the Congress?

The difficulty is this: There does not appear to be a satisfactory objective method for weighing scopes—for example, foreign policy, taxation, appropriations, public opinion, elections, and so on. Evaluating the relative importance of influence over these areas tends to be arbitrary or subjective. An analogous problem arises when we try to compare two athletes who compete in different sports. Was Babe Ruth a better athlete than Jack Dempsey? The question seems unanswerable. We might measure Babe Ruth against other hitters by using the number of home runs as a measure, and we might measure Dempsey against other fighters by using the number of knockouts, but how are home runs compared with knockouts? If two athletes were to compete in the same sports, perhaps we could determine that one was a better athlete by comparison. For example, if A were as good a hitter as B in baseball, an equally good boxer, but better in tennis, we might then say that A was a better athlete than B.

In exactly the same way it seems reasonable to say that one actor has more aggregate influence only if A's influence is not less than B's in any issue area and greater in at least one issue area. If Green and Thompson are both highly influential on public school issues and urban redevelopment but Green is more influential than Thompson on political nominations, then Green is more influential than Thompson in the aggregate.

Real life, however, does not always produce such neatly tailored situations. Green may be more influential than Thompson on school questions, while Thompson may be more influential than Green on political nominations. What do we say in this case? We might try to assign weights to different issue areas, but weights are bound to be arbitrary. If schools are given a weight of 1, what weight should be given to political nominations—2, 5, ½? How can we justify the weights we assign?

It might be thought that the total size of an actor's domain could provide a measure of his total power. But we can see that this would lead to absurdities in comparing the total power of different actors, because it would ignore both the amount of power within a given scope and the incomparability of influence within different scopes. Thus, if Green can mobilize 5,000 votes for any candidate he supports and Thompson 10,000, it seems reasonable to say that Thompson's influence on elections is greater than Green's. But suppose that Green can always mobilize 6 votes on the eleven-person city council while Thompson can mobilize none. It would then be silly to insist that because Thompson's 10,000 votes outnumber Green's 5,000 votes, therefore Thompson's total power is greater than Green's.

There is at present no single best way of solving the problem of comparability when actors have different amounts of influence with respect to different matters. Perhaps the most important lesson the student of politics can gain from this is the need for caution and clarity in making comparisons of influence. As in many other cases, it is wise in political analysis to specify whether we are adding oranges, or apples, or oranges *and* apples.

OBSERVING INFLUENCE

At this point the impatient reader might ask: If these measures are so difficult to apply in practice, how am I ever going to learn anything by trying to observe influence in the real world—in Congress, for example? The answer is that the formal notions of influence and ways of measuring relative influence serve as guides to observation and analysis. They constitute criteria that can rarely be met perfectly and often only crudely.

The best political observers ask essentially those questions suggested by our semantic analysis so far. For example, they may ask: What persons or groups have the greatest effect on congressional legislation of taxes? Who tends to initiate proposals, to win others over to them, to carry them through over opposition, to veto or sidetrack the proposals of others? Why do some questions never become public issues? Although descriptions of patterns of influence were once primarily the province of journalists and historians, the last several decades have seen a flourishing of scholarly efforts by social scientists to study concrete, contemporary systems of influence—mainly at the local level.[16]

Although most studies have focused more on manifest than implicit influence, some investigations have observed the importance of anticipated reactions in the electoral process and hence on the influence exercised by voters and campaign contributors over elected officials. Thus Mayhew has shown recently that a substantial amount of the behavior,

[16]See, for example, Charles M. Bonjean, Terry N. Clark, and Robert L. Lineberry, eds., *Community Politics: A Behavioral Approach* (New York: Free Press, 1971).

processes, and policies of members of the United States Congress can be explained adequately by the Representative's or Senator's desire for re-election.[17] Tufte has shown that federal expenditures usually increase during election years and increase more during presidential election years than during the mid-term congressional election years. These election-year increases are not accidental; they result from pressures exerted by the President and his party associates in the Executive Branch and the Congress in order to create a favorable partisan climate for the coming election.[18]

EXPLAINING DIFFERENCES IN INFLUENCE

However crude or imperfect our observations may be, one of the most commonly reported characteristics of all political systems is that political influence is unequally distributed. Why is this so? Assuming that we have observed and described the way influence is distributed among the members of some political system, how could we explain what we had found? In general, differences in the amount of influence that persons exercise can be attributed directly to three fundamental explanatory factors:

1. Differences in the distribution of political resources. A political resource is a means by which one person can influence the behavior of other persons; political resources therefore include money, information, food, the threat of force, jobs, friendship, social standing, the right to make laws, votes, as well as a great variety of other things.
2. Variations in the skill or efficiency with which individuals use their political resources. Differences in political skill stem in turn from differences in endowments, opportunities, and incentives to learn and practice political skills.
3. Variations in the extent to which individuals use their resources for political purposes. Of two equally wealthy people, for example, one may use her wealth to gain influence while another may use his to achieve success in business. These variations are themselves traceable to differences in motivations that arise out of variations in endowments and experiences.

The Network of Causes

Thus some key links in the causal network might be illustrated by Figure 5. These links are only a part of the network of causation. Other links radiate indefinitely beyond this immediate focus. The analysis of influence is similar to other causal analysis. How do we explain a particular

[17]David R. Mayhew, *Congress: The Electoral Connection* (New Haven: Yale University Press, 1974).
[18]Edward R. Tufte, "The Political Manipulation of the Economy; Influence of the Electoral Cycle on Macroeconomic Performance and Policy" (forthcoming).

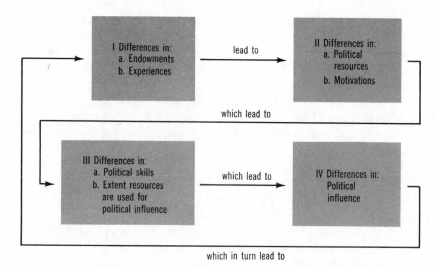

Figure 5

forest fire? If we conclude that it was caused by a camper, why did the camper cause the fire? Did he deliberately set it? If so, why did he wish to set fire to the forest? If his action was not deliberate, how do we explain his carelessness? What about other causes? Were the woods unusually dry? If so, why? Shall we also try to explain the peculiar weather? Is this likely to be a long-run cycle? Why didn't the Park Service prevent camping during the dry period?

The links on which we focus attention in a causal explanation depend on our purposes and interests. Perhaps we want to understand why campers are careless with fires in the hopes that a program of public information or regulation might help. Or we may want to determine how the Park Service can prevent fire. We may also want to consider changing the weather by cloud-seeding during dry periods. If complete analysis required us to trace every cause back to its causes, with an indefinitely widening network of causes, then a complete analysis of forest fires would be impossible.

So, too, with the analysis of influence. Where we wish to bring our inquiry to a halt depends upon our interests. Returning to Figure 4 for a moment, are we primarily interested in explaining the consequences [d] of the President's actions or the actions themselves [b] and [c]? If we choose consequences, are we concerned primarily with the role of the President, with the thought that we might shift these decisions to an independent body? Or are we interested primarily in the relationship between the milk producers and the President, with the thought or regulating campaign contributions? Or are we interested in how certain inequalities in resources, skills, and incentives lead to certain decisions with consequences that reinforce the inequalities?

We may wish to focus on still other linkages. For example, if we want to explain why certain decision-makers, such as the President, make the decisions they do, we could examine the effects of:

Their current values, attitudes, expectations, and information

Their earlier or more fundamental attitudes, values, beliefs, ideologies, personality structures, predispositions

The values, attitudes, expectations, information, beliefs, ideologies, and personalities of others whose actions are in some way relevant to the decision

The process of selection, recruitment, or entry by which decision-makers arrive at their positions

The rules of decision-making they follow, the political structures, the constitutional system

The other institutions of the society, the economic, social, religious, cultural, and educational structures that allocate key resources

The prevailing culture, particularly the political culture

The historical events that influenced the culture, institutions, structures

And so on.

No doubt a complete explanation of influence relations in a political system would try to describe and explain effects attributable to all these links in the chain of social causation, and others as well. Yet this is such a staggering task that it might well serve as a program for all the social sciences for generations. Meanwhile, it is important to specify the links in the chain one is studying. A good deal of confusion and controversy are produced when analysts focus on different links in the chain of power and causation without clearly specifying what effects they wish to explain. A good deal of criticism of dubious relevance is produced by critics who hold that the investigator has focused on the "wrong" links or did not provide a "complete" explanation. The problem is not that there are two faces of power rather than one, as some writers contend,[19] even that there are three faces rather than two.[20] The problem is that there are an indefinite number of critical links in the chain of causation and therefore an indefinite number of "faces" of power.[21]

[19]Peter Bachrach and Morton Baratz, "The Two Faces of Power," *American Political Science Review* vol. 56 (1962), pp. 947–52.

[20]Steven Lukes, *Power: A Radical View* (London: Macmillan & Co., 1974).

[21]Some of the problems are represented by conflicting interpretations in Steven Rosen, ed., *Testing the Theory of the Military-Industrial Complex* (Boston: D. C. Heath & Co., 1973).

AUTONOMY AND THE PRIME MOVERS

The logical complement of influence is autonomy. To the extent that A influences B on some matter X, then B is not autonomous in relation to A with respect to X. Conversely, B is autonomous in relation to A, with respect to X, to the extent that A does not influence B's actions or intentions with respect to X. If Albert cannot influence Barbara, his supervisor, to grant him an extra week's vacation in the summer, then by definition Barbara is autonomous in relation to Albert with respect to the matter of the vacation. Barbara, of course, may not be autonomous on this matter in relation to actors other than Albert. For example, her decision on Albert's vacation may be completely controlled by Arthur, the general manager.

In an isolated and comparatively small system we might discover actors who are autonomous in relation to all other actors on matters of crucial importance. These would be the "prime movers." They are no doubt what we consider "the center of power," "the ruling group," "the power structure," and so on. But in systems that are not small and isolated, discovering prime movers is difficult and may be impossible. Chains of causation extend indefinitely outward and indefinitely backward in time, to include other actors who influence the actors who influence the actors who . . . ad infinitum. In these cases, the network of causation is an indefinitely expanding universe.

The indefinite expansibility of causal networks poses problems not only for the analysis of influence but also for the analysis of a great many causal systems in nature and society. In practice, whether in political analysis or the natural sciences, the indefinite expansibilities of causation can be dealt with only by deliberately specifying the boundaries of the system in which we happen to be interested. It may be enough for us to know that on most matters involving Albert's job, Arthur controls Barbara, who controls Albert. But for other purposes, we shall want to ask: Who controls Arthur on these matters?

Some conflicting interpretations contained in different analyses of power arise because actors or institutions that are interpreted as autonomous and influential vis-à-vis the other actors within a given subsystem may be interpreted as not autonomous and relatively less influential vis-à-vis actors or institutions that might be included in a larger system. This regress in the location of prime movers is most visible within hierarchical political systems such as a military unit, a government bureaucracy, a business firm, or a dictatorship. In systems like these, low-level officials are autonomous in relation to their subordinates; but in relation to their superiors they are subordinates. The regress might finally be considered to come to a halt with a set of superiors "at the top." But of course the "top" of a particular hierarchy also may not be completely autonomous: the top military officials may be influenced by the Secretary of defense, who is influenced by the President, who is influenced by. . . .

Thus government and society in a nation-state are usually far more complex than comparatively simple hierarchical systems like those of military units. Hence the prime movers are much more difficult to identify —if, indeed, they exist at all. According to Marxist theory, in capitalist societies, the capitalist class unilaterally rules over the society. In this sense the class as a whole might be considered the prime mover. But the unilateral dominance of the capitalist class is more a theoretical postulate or hypothesis than a well-verified description of contemporary nonsocialist nation-states with "democratic" governments. According to democratic theory, in democracies the people are the prime movers; but few political analysts would regard this as a satisfactory description of the actual political system of any nation-state. Indeed, in systems that are not strictly hierarchical, but operate instead with many mutual controls, there is no reason to suppose that ultimate prime movers exist.

CHAPTER FOUR

FORMS
OF
INFLUENCE

Describing the chairman of his committee, a congressman said, "I wouldn't use the term powerful. I'd say influential. There's a difference."[1]

Like the congressman, to most of us the terms influence, power, authority, and control suggest different meanings. Sometimes the nuances in meaning are subtle, even elusive. Like so much of the language of politics and political analysis, the meaning of these terms is vague, unclear, and ambiguous.

Nevertheless, political analysis would be impoverished if we were compelled to work only with the generic meaning of the term influence. Many of the "differences that make a difference" would have to be ignored if political analysis could not distinguish the different forms of influence.

Consider, for example, how differences in meaning become crucially important in these two situations:

> By making me aware of my talent as a musician, my music teacher inspired me to become a composer, and for that I owe her eternal gratitude.

> By threatening to kill me with the gun he held to my head, the thief forced me to give him the combination to the safe, and robbed me of my life savings.

[1] Quoted in John Manley, *The Politics of Finance: The House Committee on Ways and Means* (Boston: Little, Brown & Co., 1970), pp. 122–123.

42

Both are instances of influence in the generic sense of the term. But what a difference!

Although it is important to be able to make distinctions, this does not mean that we can make these distinctions simply by stipulating a number of definitions.[2] The concern of this chapter is meaning—the semantic aspect of analysis. Indeed, because of the necessity to convey meaning in political analysis, works that convey the optimum understanding of power and influence in concrete situations are often detailed, descriptive, subtle, and employ a vocabulary of variety and nuance. In this chapter attention will be called to forms of influence that make a difference to us. The distinctions will help us to understand influence even if an adequate description of a complex political system, such as a local community, would require discriminating language beyond the concepts in this chapter.

INFLUENCE: POSITIVE AND NEGATIVE

The generic relationship defined in the last chapter is referred to by different names—influence, control, power, and authority. Since the word influence accords moderately well with common usage, I propose to use it as the name for the generic relationship.

We have already seen how implicit influence may be distinguished from manifest influence. In doing so, I refrained from calling attention to one aspect of influence that might seem anomalous. To determine whether A influences B, the concept in the last chapter did not explicitly require that B must respond in a way that is favorable to A's desires.[3] One ordinarily takes this for granted. Sometimes, however, one might want to describe instances of negative influence—that is, where A causes B to respond, but against, rather than in accordance with, A's desires. It has been said, for example, that because he attacked the Marshall Plan, Stalin actually helped to gain its approval in the United States Congress.

Most of the time we are interested in positive influence. Forms of control do not have crystalline boundaries. They merge into one another. I can not offer a well-defined point on the continuum at which one form definitely becomes another. There is a problem here, but because it is one that confronts a vast amount of political and social inquiry, I do not wish

[2]In an appendix to the Italian translation of the first edition of this book, I showed how 14,000 different forms of influence could be defined!

[3]For ease of exposition, I shall continue to refer to only two actors. It should be remembered, however, that influence relationships can involve a multiplicity of actors in complex causal networks.

to stress it further. The problem is not, certainly, unique to the analysis of influence.

THE MEANS OF INFLUENCE

By definition, A controls B if A's desires cause a change in B's actions or predispositions. Differences in the means by which B's actions or preferences are altered are of crucial significance. Consider again the examples given a moment ago. To help the student realize her potentialities as a composer, the music teacher probably relied very heavily on communicating information that affected the student's perceptions of the alternatives open to her and thus changed her actions or predispositions. The thief, however, relied on changing his victim's perceptions of the alternatives by changing the alternatives themselves: both by presenting the victim with two wholly new alternatives and excluding possibilities previously available and by making sure that the balance of advantage heavily favored one alternative—yielding the combination of the safe as against the risk of being shot.

Ordinarily, when A actually changes the alternatives available to B, A also will make sure that B perceives the change. If B fails to notice the change, his understanding of the situation remains unchanged, and the action A desires may not be forthcoming. Sometimes, however, A may affect B's understanding of the situation only by communicating information to B. "Look out! That's a live wire!" is likely to be sufficient to affect B's actions if B hasn't noticed the power line in his path blown down by the recent storm. The objective alternatives are unchanged; it is still the case that B can either pay no attention to the power line and run the risk of electrocution or pay attention to it and avoid injury. A has not changed these alternatives. What he has changed is B's perceptions of the alternatives. That change has come about purely by means of A's sudden communication of new and critically important information. In the extreme case, if a person already has been trained to respond more or less automatically to specific stimuli—such as a command, order, or request—the aspect of the communication that brings about B's actions is devoid of information about rewards. B simply responds in a way that he has learned is appropriate to this particular sign, signal, cue, or stimulus.

In practice, of course, a relationship of influence may depend upon a combination of these different means. Nonetheless, in order to clarify the critical differences among possible means of influence, it is useful to distinguish between means in the following way. Influence through communication that consists of a cue or signal might be called *control by training.* Influence by means of communications that provide information (correct or misleading) about the advantages and disadvantages of alternative courses of action can be called *persuasion.* Influence by means that bring about a change in the nature of the alternatives themselves by adding advantages to an alternative or imposing new disadvantages on an alternative, or both, can be called *inducement.*

Persuasion and inducement are themselves broad categories. Each contains subtypes of such great practical and moral difference that the distinctions have been emphasized since Socrates in all forms of political analysis, no matter whether the emphasis is primarily empirical, normative, policy, or semantic.

Trained Control

A common assumption is that learning comes about (whether exclusively so or not) through reinforcement of particular actions by means of rewards. This view contends that habitual responses are those that have been satisfactorily reinforced in the past. On this assumption, then, trained control is a product of prior persuasion and inducements. Yet once B is trained, then persuasion and inducement become unnecessary, except for occasional reinforcement or retraining.

Because the initial period of training requires persuasions and inducements, trained control is not costless. But once the training is completed, the costs of trained control are ordinarily very low, for they consist of the costs of communicating the necessary cues or signals. Moreover, a large share of the costs of trained control is often borne not by the actor currently exercising control, but by the social units through which the individual has already acquired much of his habituation and socialization, such as the family, peers, schools, previous work organizations, and so on.

Because it is impossible to grow up without developing habitual responses, a considerable element of trained control exists in every society. It may be that there is some component of trained control in most enduring relations of influence. It is, certainly, a ubiquitous form of influence.

Persuasion

Rational Persuasion. One form of persuasion that often is singled out as humane and desirable takes place by means of rational communication —a successful effort by A to enable B to come to an understanding of his "true" situation by means of truthful information. Persuasion by rational communication (*rational persuasion*) is consistent with Kant's moral injunction that one should treat other human beings always as ends in themselves, never as means to an end. In this respect, some people might object to conceiving of rational persuasion as influence at all. Yet it is, as a few examples will show.

A physician warns a patient: "If you don't stop smoking three packs of cigarettes a day, you will run a high risk of lung cancer. And you certainly aren't doing your weak heart any good either." A lawyer advises a client: "My best judgment is that if you take this to court, you'll lose." An architect apologizes: "I'm sorry, but I've costed out the house you had in mind, and it is going to cost you at least twice the figure you stipulated as your outside limit." In each case, if the client responds to the alternatives in the light of this new information, the physician, lawyer, or architect has caused the client to do something that he otherwise would not have chosen to do. In terms of influence, the desires of the professional have affected the client's actions or predispositions to act.

It is no accident that the examples I have chosen are all drawn from relations between professionals and clients. A professional code of conduct is intended to require that in relationships with the client, the professional transmits only information that is, to the best of her knowledge, truthful.

Manipulative Persuasion. Rational persuasion represents rational communication in its purest form. But there are many dishonest forms of communication in which there is no intention of transmitting only truthful information. Persuasion can be deliberately deceptive. Here A seeks to persuade B to act not by providing a correct understanding of the alternatives based upon truthful information but by means of manipulating B's understanding. Manipulative persuasion exists when A influences B by communication that intentionally distorts, falsifies, or omits aspects of the truth known to A but not significant and relevant to B's decision.

Unlike rational persuasion, manipulative persuasion is inconsistent with Kant's moral imperative: In manipulative persuasion persons are treated not as ends but as means, instruments, or subjects. Although manipulative persuasion usually is thought to occupy a moral standing far beneath rational persuasion, in philosophical and ideological statements great ends are not infrequently held to justify intrinsically bad means. Thus Plato recommended manipulative persuasion in order to establish his ideal Republic.[4] Political movements across the spectrum from Left to Right have followed Plato's footsteps. Former President Nixon and his advisers justified the great Watergate cover-up on these grounds.

Inducement

Often when A wishes to control B with respect to some scope of activity, it is insufficient for A to communicate information—truthful or deceptive

---

[4]Allan Bloom, trans., *The Republic of Plato,* with notes and an interpretive essay (New York: Basic Books, 1968), pp. 93–94.

—about the alternatives B supposedly confronts. An employer who warns an employee, "If you go on strike, you'll lose your wages" ordinarily would be telling the truth, but the employee might nonetheless choose to strike. The employer might try to manipulate an employee's understanding by dubious truth or even by outright lies: "Look, if you go on strike you'll never get another job with this company." Yet the employer might still fail to persuade a worker who believes that her wages are too low, and therefore she will join her fellow workers in a strike for higher wages. The employer might prefer to avoid a strike altogether by giving in to a wage raise, thus inducing the employees to stay on the job. The employer influences the employee by changing the nature of the alternatives themselves: he adds to the attractiveness of remaining on the job in comparison with striking.

In comparison with rational persuasion, which is generally considered a good means of influence, and manipulative persuasion, which is widely condemned (although widely practiced), influence by means of rewards has no definite moral standing one way or another. Nearly everyone, I imagine, considers positive inducements good in some situations and bad in others. To judge whether the employer is right to offer employees higher pay not to strike and whether an employee is right to accept it, would require a thorough analysis of the situation and a social-political perspective, an ideology or a political philosophy, that would provide grounds for arriving at a judgment.

Power. With other kinds of influence by inducements, however, the ethical questions are more acute and direct. Suppose, for example, that an employer says: "A strike is in violation of the company's contract with the union. If you go on strike, I'll get an injunction and within twenty-four hours you'll be in jail." In addition suppose that this is a truthful statement. Whereas in the preceding example the employer changed the employee's preference ordering by adding an alternative consisting of a positive inducement, in this example the employer modifies an existing alternative—to strike—by adding the prospect of severe punishment. Influence of this kind, when compliance is attained by creating the prospect of severe sanctions for noncompliance, is often called power.[5]

---

[5]This accords with the definition of Harold D. Lasswell and Abraham Kaplan, in *Power and Society* (New Haven: Yale University Press, 1950): "A *decision* is a policy involving severe sanctions (deprivations). . . . *Power* is participation in the making of decisions. . . . It is the threat of sanctions which differentiates power from influence in general. Power is a special case of the exercise of influence: it is the process of affecting policies of others with the help of (actual of threatened) severe deprivations for nonconformity with the policies intended." Lasswell cites as comparable John Locke's use of the term in the *Two Treatises of Government* (1960): "Political Power, then, I take to be a right of making laws, with penalties of death, and consequently all less penalties" pp. 74–76.

Such a conception of power may have been in the minds of members of the Ways and Means Committee who denied that their chairman, Wilbur Mills, exercised "power" over them:

> Power—you mean influence? In the sense of influence? I agree with that. He's considerate. He's as considerate of the most junior member as he is of the most senior. That's why he's "powerful."

> I wouldn't use the term powerful, I'd say influential. There's a difference. I'll compare him with . . . Carl Vinson. Carl had power and he used it, he wasn't afraid to use it. Mills is different. He has influence. I don't mean influence in the sense you peddle influence. It isn't "you do this for me" or on a committee assignment . . . He can always bring you together. He has such great respect and influence.[6]

Exactly what constitutes a "severe" loss or deprivation is somewhat arbitrary. What a person regards as severe varies with his experiences, culture, bodily conditions, and so on. Nonetheless, probably among all peoples, exile, imprisonment, and death are considered severe punishments. Therefore, whoever can impose penalties like these is bound to be important. Indeed, the State is distinguishable from other political systems only to the extent that it successfully upholds the claim to the exclusive right to determine the conditions under which severe penalties —those involving serious physical pain, constraint, punishment, or death —may be legitimately employed.

Coercion. Suppose that Carson, another employee, desperately wants to go on working. His wife is ill, he has staggering medical expenses, his unpaid bills are overwhelming, he is about to sell his car and his house to scrape up cash—and the union has no strike fund. In these circumstances, Carson's preferences are, from best to worst:

1. To go on working at the same pay
2. To quit and find another job
3. To strike

But let us suppose that the labor union has been taken over by criminal elements who use the strike weapon to extort protection money from business firms. Allston, a union agent, threatens: "Carson, if you don't go on strike, and try to go through our picket line, we'll beat you to a pulp. And don't think you can sneak off and get another job either. Your kids

---

[6]Manley, *The Politics of Finance*, pp. 122–123. Manley, it should be said, interprets these remarks as implying a difference between a one-way relationship (power) and a "mutual process of stimulation" (influence).

might just have an accident on the way to school. You're going to join the strike—or else." After thinking it over, Carson now feels that his only alternatives are, from best to worst:

1. To strike
2. To go on working [and be badly beaten up]
3. To quit [and have his children injured]

Carson is caught. From his point of view, his options are all unsatisfactory. He is compelled to do what he had not wanted to do at all because the only remaining alternatives are much worse. If he tried to explain his situation, Carson might say, "I don't want to strike but I *have* to. I have no choice. They're forcing me to do it." In this situation, a philosopher might say that Carson is coerced.

In this instance their relationship involves a particularly sinister form of power because all the options open to Carson entail severe sanctions. No matter what he does, Carson will be a good deal worse off. He is compelled to choose a damaging alternative because all the others are even worse. This is coercion. The classic case of coercion is the one illustrated at the beginning of this chapter: "Your money or your life!"

Just as power is a form of influence, so coercion is a form of power. But not all power is strictly coercive in the sense just defined. If positive inducements are combined with severe sanctions to bring about the action desired, the relationship is one of power but not of coercion in the strict sense.

Physical Force. Power and coercion do not necessarily require the use or threat of physical force. However, physical force is often involved in power and coercion, although it is an inefficient form of influence, too clumsy and costly for most purposes. Despots may rule by fear, but never only by force. Even a despot needs guards, jailers, and a military that is loyal and obedient. And the despot himself cannot directly force every soldier, jailer, or guard to comply with his wishes.

What makes coercion effective is not the actual use of physical force, rather it is the threat to harm another by physical force if the other does not comply. The threat of force often makes coercion an effective goal or deterrent to action. The actual use of force occasionally may help make the threat credible. But if the threat must always be carried out, coercion by force becomes self-defeating. A thief may turn a live victim into a dead one; but a corpse cannot open the safe. If the great powers should ever carry out the threat of nuclear war, there may be no survivors. The actual employment of physical force, then, usually signifies that a policy based on the threat of force has failed.

Unilateral and Reciprocal Control

Control is not necessarily one-way or unilateral. It may also be mutual or reciprocal. Consider a discussion in which each person influences the others by rational persuasion. Or imagine a congressman who always seeks to vote on legislation according to what will most please his constituents. In his voting decisions, then, he is firmly under the control of his constituents by means of anticipated reactions. But, if he is untiring and successful in his efforts to keep them accurately informed of what he is doing for them, then he in turn may influence them by rational persuasion to vote for him at the next election.

Exchanges or transactions, which are as ubiquitous in political as in economic life, appear always to involve mutual control: each party to an exchange modifies his or her actions in response to the offers or promises of the other.

Perhaps the most consequential contemporary instance of reciprocal control is the system of mutual deterrence that has helped to prevent nuclear war. The leaders of each country make their decisions in anticipation of the probable response of the other country's leaders. Since each set of leaders anticipates their own country's destruction in a nuclear war, each side chooses alternatives that do not involve the use or the immediate threat of using nuclear weapons. While the leaders of the Soviet Union and the United States are autonomous in relation to one another on most decisions they make, on military and diplomatic decisions they are involved in a system of reciprocal control. It is fragile but of unparalleled importance for survival.

EVALUATING FORMS OF INFLUENCE

These distinctions are important to us because of their moral and practical significance. Most of us tend to regard rational persuasion, for example, as more desirable than coercion. To make a thoughtful evaluation of the different forms of influence is no easy matter. I can do no more here than to offer a few suggestions that ought to be considered an introduction and not a conclusion to the subject.

Among the forms of influence, rational persuasion may have a claim to a unique moral standing. The grounds for such acclaim would be something like this: Because by definition the only means it employs is the accurate communication of information believed to be strictly true, rational persuasion is a form of enlightenment. To the extent that the information conveyed by rational persuasion is in fact true, it cannot be intrinsically harmful to the other. It may forecast possible harm: "If you do not stop smoking, you may incur lung cancer." But rational persuasion is itself intrinsically neutral: by itself it neither adds to nor subtracts from the good of the other. It is, however, desirable instrumentally (or extrinsically) because through enlightenment it may bring about the good of the other: armed with knowledge acquired through rational communication the other may now choose the better rather than the worse alternative—or, at the least, accept the inevitable.

It is no accident, then, that a notion of mutual influence based on rational persuasion lies often half-hidden in the heart of many conceptions of an ideal society. In the eyes of many Athenians, an ideal polis might well have had this quality. Influence in the assembly by gifted leaders like Pericles would rest solely on their exceptional capacity for rational persuasion. Rousseau's conception of a republic in which every citizen is morally free and yet bound by laws of his own choosing also partakes of this idea. Citizens engage in mutual, rational persuasion and accept freely the obligations created by the collective decisions taken at the conclusion of the discussion. This is an implicit ideal in a great deal of democratic thought. It is often an even more explicit ideal in anarchist thought.

Yet no large number of persons has ever interacted over an extended period of time in and outside their group without developing means of influence other than rational persuasion.

Manipulative persuasion, power, coercion, the threat and application of physical force are commonplace aspects of political life. Every State uses power internally to secure compliance with the policies of the Government. Manipulative persuasion, power, coercion, and physical force have been common in the relations among states; in international politics, war or the threat of war has frequently been used as an alternative to stalemate or peaceful adjustment. Civil wars and revolutions also involve power and coercion; each side resorts to physical force to impose its will on others. It is easy for people accustomed to relatively stable political systems like those of Britain and the United States to lose sight of the frequency of revolutions, civil wars, and violence. Even today, in large parts of the world, civil strife, guerrilla warfare, revolutionary struggles, violence, and suppression of political opponents by physical force are normal and commonplace political practices. It may help Americans to understand the pervasiveness of "internal war" if they remember that our Civil War lasted five years and was one of the bloodiest exhibitions of fratricide in modern history.

Although these things happen, this is not to say that they are morally justified. One might ask, then, whether anything other than rational persuasion can ever be morally justified. After all, manipulative persuasion violates a fundamental and widespread ethical injunction that favors truth over lying. Power, particularly in the form of coercion and where physical force is employed, involves the prospect of inflicting pain on another person, sometimes even causing death. Thus power may be, and coercion surely is, intrinsically harmful.

To avoid intrinsically undesirable means, one might conclude that the only morally permissible means of influence is rational persuasion. Let me call this the *absolute principle* of rational persuasion. Yet this solution immediately leads to self-contradiction unless it is universally adopted. Suppose that some persons use manipulative persuasion or coercion to get what they want. How are we now to apply the principle of rational persuasion? On the one hand, we might conclude that the principle enjoins us to use only rational persuasion in order to dissuade the violators of that principle. Yet if rational persuasion proves ineffectual, as it will in many cases, then we have no effective way of upholding our principle in practice. Alternatively, then, in order to enforce our principle, we might punish or threaten to punish the violators of that principle. But in this case we ourselves will have violated the principle.

Because of this dilemma, it appears that the absolute principle of rational persuasion never can be upheld until it is always adhered to by everyone. Consequently, even pacifists and advocates of nonviolence are rarely prepared to extend their program to cover all situations. Few pacifists would insist that there be no laws regulating air and water pollution, driving speeds through congested areas, the sale and use of firearms, or the conduct of police or onlookers during a peaceful demonstration; or that such laws should not be enforced; or that enforcement must never involve coercive means, such as fines and imprisonment for law-breakers.

Agreement by rational persuasion for some persons can mean coercion for others. In 1787, the American Constitutional Convention negotiated a peaceful settlement of the issues surrounding the new Constitution. One of the compromises of that convention was the perpetuation of slavery. A decade after slavery was abolished as a by-product of a fearfully destructive Civil War, peaceful compromises among national leaders in Washington permitted the rapid restoration of white supremacy in the South. An opponent of slavery or white supremacy confronted, then, the alternatives of persuading white southerners to abandon their beliefs and practices, a feat that even in retrospect seems impossible; to bring about change in the South by force or the threat of force; or to permit the South to impose a dreadful coercion on its black inhabitants.

If these examples show the difficulty in adhering consistently to a position stating that the use of intrinsically undesirable means of influence are never justifiable, they do not controvert the view that some of the means we believe we must employ are intrinsically bad. They help to show, rather, the tragic dilemma that political man can face. One may or may not face this dilemma responsibly, but so far no one has discovered a way to avoid it.

A second response to this problem, then, is to hold that an action involving power and even coercion is sometimes better than any available alternative. Thus one may judge coercion to be intrinsically bad yet extrinsically or instrumentally desirable in some circumstances. This tension between the intrinsic undesirability of certain means of influence and their unavoidability as instruments is one of the most poignant and troubling problems in man's life as a social and political being.

CHAPTER FIVE

SIMILARITIES IN POLITICAL SYSTEMS

There are two extreme but common views about political systems. According to one, political systems never vary in their important aspects. According to the other, they are so plastic that they can be molded to suit the heart's desire.

Even if, as is the case with practically all disagreements about politics, some of the differences in these perspectives are purely semantic, at base the conflict is more than a matter of words. Consider, for example, the hypothesis that all political systems are dominated by a ruling class or ruling elite, a view associated with three men whose lives spanned the tumultuous changes in Europe during the last quarter of the nineteenth century and the first quarter of the twentieth. Two were eminent Italians: Vilfredo Pareto (1848–1923) and Gaetano Mosca (1858–1941); the third, who was of German birth, lived much of his life in Italy: Roberto Michels (1876–1936). All three achieved acclaim among social theorists disillusioned with or cynical about democracy. A statement by Mosca seems to catch the essence of their argument:

> Among the constant facts and tendencies that are to be found in all political organisms, one is so obvious that it is apparent to the most casual eye. In all societies—from societies that are very meagerly developed and have barely attained the dawnings of civilization, down to the most advanced and powerful societies—two classes of people appear—a class that rules and a class that is ruled. The first class, always the less numerous, performs all political functions, monopolizes power and enjoys the advantages that

power brings, whereas the second, the more numerous class, is directed and controlled by the first, in a manner that is now more or less legal, now more or less arbitrary and violent, and supplies the first, in appearance at least, with material means of subsistence and with the instrumentalities that are essential to the vitality of the political organism.[1]

At the opposite extreme are naïve (but not always youthful) enthusiasts poised on the eve of Utopia's arrival, who proclaim, and may even believe, that when the New Day dawns "politics" will disappear. Observers disagree about what is persistent in politics and what is open to change, and it would be misleading to suggest that in our present state of knowledge the matter can be firmly settled. Each of the extreme views incorporates some of the truth, but each is also incomplete.

As to the view that politics is infinitely plastic, a multitude of experience—most recently that of newly independent nations—shows that after the sun rises on a new society without politics, by high noon the "old" politics has returned with a vengeance. By some standards the new politics may be better, perhaps very much better, than the old—or it may be worse, perhaps very much worse: but in at least some respects the two will be very much alike.

It is these similarities, these stubborn and until now apparently inescapable regularities, to which I wish to call your attention in this chapter.

A Prior Question: How Many? Just how many political systems are there in the world? No one knows. Given the broad definition of "political system" used here, they must number in the millions. In 1968 there were about 136 independent countries and 62 colonies and other dependencies—mainly islands. In one country, the United States, there were 50 states, 3,043 counties, 17,996 muncipalities, 17,144 townships and towns, 34,678 independent school districts, and 18,322 special districts,

[1]Mosca, *The Ruling Class (Elementi di Scienza Politica,* 1896), ed. Arthur Livingston (New York: McGraw-Hill Book Co., 1939), p. 50. (Copyright 1939 by McGraw-Hill. Used by permission of McGraw-Hill Book Company.) The hypothesis is also set forth by Pareto in The Mind and Society (*Trattato di Sociologia Generale,* 1916), 4 vols. (New York: Harcourt Brace Jovanovich, 1935), in vol. 4, p. 1569), and by Michels, *Political Parties* (1915) (New York: Collier Books, 1962), p. 342 ff. A superb study of Mosca that includes as an appendix the final version of his theory of the ruling class is James H. Meisel, *The Myth of the Ruling Class* (Ann Arbor: University of Michigan Press, 1956). An excellent introduction to Pareto will be found in *Vilfredo Pareto: Sociological Writings,* selected and introduced by S. E. Finer (New York: Praeger, 1966). See also S. E. Finer, "Pareto and Pluto-Democracy: The Retreat to Galapagos," *American Political Science Review* 62 (June 1968): 440–450. A succinct summary and critique of Michels is John D. May's "Democracy, Organization, Michels," *American Political Science Review,* 59 (June 1965): 417–429.

not to speak of uncounted business firms, trade unions, families, and voluntary associations.[2]

Our systematic knowledge extends to only a small portion of the behavior of a tiny number of these systems. Political science advances through the specialized study of particular types of political system. What we are seeking in this chapter, however, are the characteristics of political systems in general, or, at any rate, in systems involving more than a handful of people. Remember: these similarities are not a part of the definition of a political system. They are regularities—empirical regularities, one might say—that one can expect to find in any large political system.

CHARACTERISTICS OF POLITICAL SYSTEMS

Uneven Control of Political Resources. Control over political resources is distributed unevenly. There are four reasons why this is so.

(1) Some specialization of function exists in every society; in advanced societies specialization is extensive. Specialization of function (the division of labor) creates differences in access to different political resources. A Secretary of State and a member of the Senate Foreign Relations Committee have much more access to information about American foreign policy than do most citizens. An officers' cabal in Panama has more opportunity to use the threat of force to gain its ends than does a conspiracy among schoolteachers.

(2) Because of inherited differences, all people do not start life with the same access to resources, and those with a head start often increase their lead. Individuals and societies are to some extent prisoners of the past; they never start with a completely clean slate either biologically or socially. Some endowments are biological. Many endowments, such as wealth, social standing, or the level of education and aspiration of one's parents, are not biological, however, but social. Whatever their source, differences in biological and social endowments at birth often multiply into even greater differences in resources among adults. Almost everywhere, for example, opportunities for education are related at least in part to the wealth, social standing, or political position of one's parents.

(3) Differences in biological and social inheritance, together with differences in experiences, all produce differences in the incentives and goals of different people in a society. As a practical matter, it is impossible

[2]These figures are from J. David Singer, Bruce M. Russett, and Melvin Small, "National Political Units in the Twentieth Century: A Standardized List," *American Political Science Review*, 62 (September 1968): (932–952; and Committee for Economic development, *Modernizing Local Government* (New York: C.E.D., 1966), Table 3, p. 27.

for any society to provide everyone with a standard set of identical motives and aims, a kind of Do-It-Yourself Conformity Kit. Differences in motivation in turn lead to differences in skills and in resources: not everyone is equally motivated to go into politics, to become a leader, or to acquire the resources that help the leader gain influence over others.

(4) Finally, some differences in incentives and goals usually are encouraged in societies in order to equip individuals for different specialities. If everyone wanted to be a full-time warrior, who would tend the herds or crops? The circle is complete: whenever specialization of function is regarded as advantageous, some differences in motivations are also thought to be beneficial. But differences in motivations are likely to lead to differences in resources—for example, to greater military prowess for warriors than for shepherds.

For these four reasons³ it appears to be impossible to create a society in which political resources would be distributed with perfect equality among adults. However: you must not conclude that there are no important differences in the way political resources are distributed in different societies. For there are differences and they are important. That is a matter for the next chapter.

The Quest for Political Influence. *Some members of the political system seek to gain influence over the policies, rules, and decisions enforced by the government —i.e., political influence.* People seek political influence not necessarily for its own sake, but because control over the government helps them to achieve one or more of their goals. Control over the government is such a familiar way of furthering one's goals or values that it is hard to imagine a political system in which no one sought power. We know from Ruth Benedict's *Patterns of Culture* that the Zuñi Indians of the Southwest not only made no effort to gain power but even avoided it. As a result, they developed an elaborate ritual for imposing the obligations of office on a reluctant member. But this situation is as rare as General Sherman's famous disclaimer, "If nominated, I shall not run, and if elected I shall not serve."

Once again, by way of warning: don't leap to the conclusion that everyone who seeks political influence does so simply out of a desire for power as such. Although this conclusion is commonplace, the evidence against it is overwhelming. (We return to this question in Chapter 8.)

Uneven Distribution of Political Influence. *Political influence is distributed unevenly among the members of a political system.* Clearly this proposi-

³For a comprehensive treatment, see Gerhard Lenski, *Power and Privilege* (New York: McGraw-Hill Book Co., 1966), especially Chapter Four.

tion is closely related to the first one, which dealt with resources. For the fact that some people have more resources with which they can influence the Government makes it easier for them to gain more influence over the Government if and when they wish to do so. People with more influence over the Government can use their influence to gain control over more political resources.

The existence of unequal political influence has been observed for centuries; yet although many observers agree on the fact, they disagree in appraising it, some of them justifying it and others attacking it. The opening book of Aristotle's *Politics* sought to explain and justify the differences in the authority of master and slave, husband and wife, parent and child. Twenty centuries later, in the midst of the Enlightenment, Rousseau sought to explain and to attack inequalities of power in his famous essay, *A Discourse on the Origins of Inequality* (1755). Rousseau traced the origins of inequalities of power to inequalities in property. Inequality in property, he maintained, led in turn to inequalities in other resources. Less than a century after Rousseau, Marx and Engels put forth a similar explanation in the *Communist Manifesto* and a series of revolutionary works that followed. Interest in the origins of political inequality contains unabated to the present day. In 1938 Gunnar Landtman, a Finnish anthropologist, followed Rousseau's path by searching for explanations of inequality in an exhaustive examination of preliterate societies; his book bore a title that suggests both Rousseau and Marx: *The Origin of the Inequality of the Social Classes.* In 1951 an American political scientist, David Truman, observed:

> Writers of the most diverse political views and using the most widely variant methods of observation have called attention to the existence in almost all groups of an active minority—identified by such condemnatory terms as "oligarchy" and "Old Guard" or such approving ones as "public-spirited citizens" and "civic leaders."[4]

Sometimes the proposition that political influence is distributed unequally is confused with Mosca's hypothesis that in every political system there is a ruling class. But the one does not imply the other. We shall come back to this distinction in the next chapter, for the presence or absence of a ruling class is one respect in which political systems differ. It true, though, that if we call the individuals with the greatest political influence the political leaders, then our third proposition implies that every political system has political leaders. And that is the sense in which

[4] *The Governmental Process* (New York: Alfred A. Knopf, 1951), p. 139.

we shall use the term "leader" or "political leader" in this book: to refer to those individuals who have the greatest influence in a political system.

The Pursuit and Resolution of Conflicting Aims. *Members of a political system pursue conflicting aims, which are dealt with, among other means, by the government of the political system.* Conflict and consensus are both important aspects of political systems. People who live together never agree about everything, but if they are to continue to live together, they cannot wholly disagree in their aims.

Although political theorists have recognized this duality, some have placed more stress on the one than the other. Some, like Hobbes, have emphasized the propensity of men to conflict with one another; others, like Aristotle and Rousseau, their propensity for agreement and cooperation. Political theorists who, like Hobbes, emphasize the tendency of men to pursue conflicting aims are prone to stress the need for concentrated power and authority, obedience, loyalty, conformity, obligation, duty, and discipline. Theorists who, like Aristotle or Rousseau, emphasize man's immense talent for cooperation are more likely to stress how a political system, and particularly the State, can help human beings to pursue common goals, to win dignity and mutual respect, to share freedom, and to behave responsibly. Extreme views on the likelihood of cooperation and conflict usually are accompanied by extreme views about the State. Extreme fear of civic conflict is characteristic of authoritarian patterns of thought. At the other extreme, philosophical anarchists express unlimited confidence in man's cooperative nature.

The Government does not necessarily intervene every time the aims and acts of different individuals conflict. Conflict is often dealt with by nonpolitical means—by gossip, for example, or sorcery, or aggressive language, or even by isolated outbursts of violence. In many societies some form of personal combat is regarded as a normal way for men to deal with serious personal disagreements. Fistfights were a common occurrence along the American frontier, and in some places they are commonplace even today.

In complex societies a good deal of conflict is mediated, arbitrated, suppressed, resolved, or handled in some fashion by political systems other than the State. Whenever a degree of coercion is required that goes beyond what is possible or permitted to other governments operating in the territorial area of the State, officials of the Government can use their superior power by virtue of the Government's exclusive control over the conditions under which violence may be legitimately employed. Thus the Government steps in whenever the conflict is considered beyond adjustments by nonpolitical means or by other governments than that of the State. In the United States, for example, the Government does not ordinarily intervene in labor disputes. But when prolonged conflicts between a union and management in a major industry such as steel threaten to weaken the economy, the President is likely to intervene.

The Acquisition of Legitimacy. *Leaders in a political system try to ensure that whenever governmental means are used to deal with conflict, the decisions arrived at are widely accepted not solely from fear of violence, punishment, or coercion but also from a belief that it is morally right and proper to do so.* According to one usage of the term, a government is said to be "legitimate" if the people to whom its orders are directed believe that the structure, procedures, acts, decisions, policies, officials, or leaders of government possess the quality of "rightness," propriety, or moral goodness—the right, in short, to make binding rules. Thus, our fourth proposition is equivalent to saying: Leaders in a political system try to endow their actions with legitimacy.

When a leader's influence is clothed with legitimacy, it usually is referred to as authority. Authority, then, is a special kind of influence, legitimate influence. Hence, our fourth proposition is also equaivalent to: Leaders in a political system try to convert their influence into authority. Because they often succeed, the phenomena of legitimacy are widespread and important. A writer as far-ranging in his curiosity as Max Weber saw fit to concern himself almost exclusively with legitimate governments and authority, evidently in the belief that power without legitimacy was too rare to be worth studying.

It is easy to see why leaders strive for legitimacy. Authority is a highly efficient form of influence. It is not only more reliable and durable than naked coercion but it also enables a ruler to govern with a minimum of political resources. It would be impossible to rely on fear and terror, for example, to carry out the complex tasks of a large, modern, bureaucratic organization such as the U.S. Post Office, the Army, Massachusetts General Hospital, General Motors, or the public school system of New York. Also it probably would be impossible, or at any rate much more costly, to rely simply on direct rewards, for this would require an unwieldy "piece-rate" system. When a subordinate regards the orders and assignments he receives as morally binding, only a relatively small expenditure of resources, usually in the form of salaries and wages, is necessary to ensure satisfactory performance.

Although many different kinds of political systems can acquire legitimacy, democracies may be more in need of it than most other systems. In the long run democracy cannot be forced on a group of people against its will; in fact, democracy is unlikely to survive when a large minority opposes it, for democratic institutions would encounter rough going if a majority always had to impose its rule on a large minority.

An enormous variety of political systems seem to have gained considerable legitimacy in various times and places. Even in the relatively democratic society of the United States, political systems that reflect quite contradictory principles of authority acquire legitimacy. For example, business firms, government agencies, and some religious associations are organized according to hierarchical rather than democratic principles. Yet many citizens who concede legitimacy to the American government because of its democratic structure also concede legitimacy to these hierarchical systems.[5] In some time and place, almost every conceivable political arrangement—feudalism, monarchy, oligarchy, hereditary aristocracy, plutocracy, representative government, direct democracy— has acquired so much legitimacy that men have volunteered their lives in its defense.

Development of an ideology. *Leaders in a political system usually espouse a set of more or less persistent, integrated doctrines that purport to explain and justify their leadership in the system.* A set of doctrines of this kind is often called a political ideology (Mosca called it a "political formula").[6] One reason why leaders develop an ideology is obvious: to endow their leadership with legitimacy—to convert their political influence into authority. And it is far more economical to rule by means of authority than by means of coercion.

Some leaders, including the highest governmental officials and their allies, usually espouse an ideology that justifies not only their own leadership but also the political system itself. Their ideology is then the official or reigning ideology. A reigning ideology indicates the moral, religious, factual, and other assumptions that are assumed to justify the system. A highly developed reigning ideology usually contains standards for appraising the organization, policies, and leaders of the system, and also an idealized description of the way in which the system actually works, a version that narrows the gap between reality and the goal prescribed by the ideology.

In the United States, the reigning political ideology is "democracy." To be sure, the depths of the commitment, the extent to which the implications of various tenets in the ideology are understood, and the willingness to apply principles to concrete cases, all vary a great deal among Americans. Whatever the discrepancies between pronouncements and behavior, however, "democracy" is clearly the reigning ideology among Americans.[7]

Despite the fact that a reigning ideology helps incumbent leaders

---

[5]However, Harry Eckstein has argued that instability is likely if there is a lack of congruence among different authority structures in the same country. See his *Division and Cohesion in Democracy: A Study of Norway* (Princeton: Princeton University Press, 1966), Appendix B and passim. And "Authority Relations and Governmental Performance: A Theoretical Framework" *Comparative Political Studies* 2 (October 1969): 283–287.

[6]Mosca, *The Ruling Class, pp. 70–71.*

[7]For some comparisons, see Jack Dennis, Leon Lindberg, Donald McCrone, and Rodney Stiefbold, "Political Socialization to Democratic Orientations in Four Western Systems," *Comparative Political Studies*, 1 (April 1968): 71–101.

acquire legitimacy, it would be highly unrealistic to conclude that the existence or content of an ideology can be completely explained by the desires of leaders to clothe their actions with legitimacy and thus to transform naked power into authority. For one thing, the fact that many people who are not leaders accept the ideology reflects a desire for explanation, an interpretation of experiences and goals, that offers meaning and purpose to life and to one's place in the universe. It would be surprising if men who for thousands of years sought to comprehend the relative motions of planets and stars did not also want to understand their own political order. Thus illiterate peasants living in conditions of great physical and psychological deprivation frequently adopt an outlook on the world that "explains" and justifies their inequality, suffering, and frustrations.[8]

Moreover, despite appearances to the contrary, leaders cannot arbitrarily invent and manipulate a reigning ideology, for once a political ideology is widely accepted in a political system, the leaders, too, become its prisoners, for they run the risk of undermining their own legitimacy if they violate its norms.

They may even find it impossible to carry out their policies. For example, in 1936 President Roosevelt was reelected by an enormous majority. When the Supreme Court declared one key New Deal measure after another unconstitutional, he resolved to overcome the hostile majority on the Court by obtaining from Congress permission to appoint six new members. But he evidently did not anticipate the resentment that such an attempt to "pack" the Court would generate, even among the people who voted for him and supported his policies. In the fall of 1936 and the winter of 1937, a sizable majority of people evidently felt that the Supreme Court should be "more liberal in reviewing New Deal measures." Yet when the President unveiled his startling proposal in February, 1937, it was at once opposed by a substantial majority in Congress and a small majority among the general public. As the debate wore on, the magnitude of the opposition both in Congress and in the country increased. By June, surveys indicated that 60 percent of the people interviewed did not want Congress to pass the legislation.[9] In July the bill was killed. Roosevelt never regained the influence he had once enjoyed over Congress on domestic matters. Indeed, during the struggle over the Court, Roosevelt's northern Republican and southern Democratic critics

[8]Mehmet Bequiraz, *Peasantry in Revolution* (Ithaca, N.Y.: Center for International Studies, Cornell University, 1966).

[9]For survey data, see Hadley Cantril, ed., *Public Opinion*, 1935–1946 (Princeton: Princeton University Press, 1951), pp. 149–151, 755–757. For Roosevelt's proposal and strategy, see Joseph Alsop and Turner Catledge, *The 168 Days* (Garden City, N.Y.: Doubleday & Co., 1938).

in Congress learned how to form a coalition against the President, and this lesson they never forgot.

It would be unrealistic, however, to assume that a reigning ideology is a unified, consistent body of beliefs accepted by everyone in a political system. In the first place, the extent to which a distinguishable ideology actually is developed and articulated varies enormously from one political system to another. Many political systems simply share the reigning ideology that lends legitimacy to the Government and the State. Thus it would be a good deal more difficult to specify the prevailing ideology among members of the United Automobile Workers or General Motors than among Americans generally. In the second place, no ideology is ever entirely integrated or internally consistent. For one thing, an ideology is not necessarily static; new situations create a need for new explanations and emphasis on new goals, and thus novel and unrelated or even inconsistent elements creep in. Then, too, a certain amount of ambiguity is sometimes a positive advantage precisely because it permits flexibility and change. The fact that the Soviet ideology is ambiguous about how and when the final condition of full communism is to be reached permits Soviet leaders more free play than they would have if it prescribed a rigid timetable of specific steps.

Third, a reigning ideology is probably never uniformly accepted by all members of a system. Many members have only rudimentary knowledge of the prevailing ideology articulated by the leaders; others may actually hold—perhaps unwittingly—a variety of private views that are at odds with the reigning ideology. For all his insight and remarkably acute observations, Tocqueville no doubt exaggerated the uniformity with which Americans subscribed to democratic ideals in the 1830s. Certainly there is great variation among Americans today. Citizens who agree that opponents should have the right to criticize the government disagree on the rights of Communists or revolutionaries to advocate changes. People who profess to believe in free speech may nonetheless favor the suppression of dissent. Moreover, for many people the reigning ideology, or any ideology at all, is too remote, too unimportant, too abstract, or too complex to grasp except in highly rudimentary form.[10]

Fourth, the reigning ideology may be rejected. Some members of a political system—communists or fascists in a democratic country, or democrats in an authoritarian country—may adhere to rival and conflicting ideologies. Because people differ in their aims, incumbent leaders rarely rule without incurring opposition, overt or covert; few systems can count on ungrudging support from all their members. Opponents of a

[10]There are now a number of excellent analyses of survey evidence bearing on these points. See, for example, Fred I. Greenstein's book in this series, *The American Party System and the American People*, Chapter Two.

regime often formulate criticism that deny the existing system its legitimacy. Often, too, critics depict an alternative that, unlike the existing system, is held to repose on a legitimate foundation.

Sometimes the revolutionary ideology of one period becomes the reigning ideology of the next. In the eighteenth century democratic doctrine was revolutionary ideology; today, it is the reigning ideology in the United States and most of western Europe. In Russia, Marxism and Leninism were revolutionary ideologies until 1917; since then they have become reigning ideologies, modified by Lenin's successors.

Since ideologies seem to rise and fall, and the reigning ideology of one system contradicts that of another, does one ideology possess just as much factual and moral validity as another? To anyone who finds the burden of choosing among conflicting views excessive, this view is seductive. But for good or ill, political appraisal is not easy. Nothing that has been said—and nothing that will be said later—supports the notion that all ideologies are equally valid.

The Impact of Other Political Systems. *The way a political system behaves is influenced by the existence of other political systems.* With occasional exceptions so rare that they can be ignored—a small and completely isolated club or tribe, for example—political systems do not exist in isolation.

Exceptional cases aside, every political system engages in foreign relations, for the actions open to one system are affected by the past or probable actions of others. A city cannot successfully ignore the existence of a national government: national governments must adapt their actions to the hard fact that other national governments, alliances, coalitions, and international organizations also exist. Even a club or a religious congregation cannot act with complete autonomy; and the leaders of a trade union must take into account the past or probable actions of business firms, other unions, and the government.

It is a curious fact that most people who portray their vision of an ideal political system ignore the limits imposed by the existence of other political systems. It is easy to imagine "the good society" if one does not bother with other, and quite possibly bad, societies that might clutter up the surrounding landscape. Consequently, political Utopias are usually portrayed without the troublesome limitations imposed by foreign relations, which are eliminated by either ignoring them entirely or solving them according to some simple plan.

In this respect the influence of Greek thought has been pernicious, for the emphasis of Greek political theorists on the virtues of a small, autonomous, self-sufficient State and their assumption that war was the natural and inevitable relation among States led them to ignore the usual problems of foreign affairs when States were not at war. In all Plato's

Dialogues, which have had an enormous impact on Western political thought, there are only a handful of references to foreign affairs. Aristotle criticized Plato for the omission. "If a polis," he wrote in *The Politics*, "is to live in a political life [involving intercourse with other states] and not a life of isolation, it is a good thing that its legislator should also pay regard to neighboring countries."[11] Yet Aristotle had little more to say about foreign relations than Plato. By contrast, in modern times the study of foreign relations has developed into a special branch of political science.[12]

But how can we distinguish foreign relations from internal politics? How, in other words, can we distinguish one political system from another? What are the "boundaries" of a political system? Fortunately, boundaries often are assigned to a political system by convention. Conventional boundaries may be geographical, in which case everyone within the geographical boundaries is considered to be "in" (even if not always "of") that particular system. Or membership may depend on some such conventional characteristic as paying dues, earning wages, or simply being listed as a member or employee. Because of the existence of understandings like these, it is easy to agree on the conventional boundaries of the United States, California, the U.S. Senate, the Supreme Court, the House of Representatives, the AFL-CIO, and the Benevolent and Protective Order of Elks.

Do boundaries of this kind rest on anything more than convention? Do they share a more general or abstract property? They do, and in political analysis we often employ this property to determine whether the conventional boundaries coincide with the "real" boundaries. For example, the People's Republic of China claims that its boundaries include Taiwan. Some Chinese leaders on Taiwan claim in effect that their boundaries include the mainland. Now, these moral, legal, or propagandistic claims would not necessarily be altered one iota by abstract political analysis. But it is possible to determine the boundaries of the political system that centers on Taiwan for purposes of analysis, regardless of whether these "analytical" boundaries are proper according to legal or moral criteria. In Chapter One we defined a political system as any persistent pattern of human relationships that significantly involves power, rule, or authority. Hence, for purposes of political analysis, a boundary can be assigned to a political system wherever there exists a sharp decline in the power of the government of the system to influence action.

The reason why the 2500-mile border between Canada and the

[11]Ernest Barker, ed., *The Politics of Aristotle* (Oxford: Oxford University Press, 1952), p. 57. Words in brackets interpolated by the editor, Ernest Barker.

[12]The subject is treated in Karl Deutsch's *International Relations* in this series.

United States is not merely a conventional line on a map but a meaningful boundary between two political systems is that the relative power of officials of the American and Canadian governments over one's actions depends very strongly on exactly which side of the border one happens to be on.

There may be many dips in the curve of power of a government; if so, many different points might be regarded as the boundaries of a political system. Which set of points a person uses to bound a system depends on the particular question under analysis. For example, "unlike many European parties, the major American parties have no formal membership procedures, or initiation ceremonies; there are no card-carrying Republicans or Democrats. Yet . . . a large majority of the electorate . . . identifies with one or the other of the major parties."[13] Depending on the problem at hand, political scientists stipulate different boundaries for the parties: the "party" may include only the leaders or activists, for example, or all registered adherents, or, for some purposes, even all party "identifiers."

One should not be disturbed if the boundaries of political systems are somewhat rubbery, for, in practice, conventional boundaries are usually sufficient. When they are not, a little attention to the problem one is trying to analyze, and some familiarity with the particular system, will usually indicate a number of satisfactory points which one can use to trace the bounds.

The Inevitability of Change. It is appropriate to close this chapter by emphasizing a regularity that anticipates the subject of the next: *All political systems undergo change.*

From time immemorial political observers have pointed out the mutability of political systems. "Seeing that everything which has a beginning has also an end," wrote Plato, "even a constitution such as yours will not last forever, but will in time be dissolved." With his characteristic preference for imaginative and somewhat rigid theoretical notions drawn from brilliant speculation but not tested against concrete experience, Plato went on to describe the inevitable process of decay through which even the perfect aristocracy he proposed must degenerate into a "timocracy," or government of honor, to be followed in succession by oligarchy, thence by democracy, and finally by tyranny.

Aristotle rejected Plato's dialectic, but he devoted a lengthy section of *The Politics* to the causes of revolutions and constitutional change; he extended the theory of political change well beyond where Plato had taken it. Because of their solid good sense, his remarks are still worth reading.

[13]Fred I. Greenstein, in *The American Party System and the American People,* in this series.

Although students of politics have observed the mutability of political systems, it is an interesting fact that those who set out to reveal the lineaments of an ideal State generally eliminate all change from their Utopia. Being perfect, the ideal State either cannot change or, if it changes at all, must change for the worse. Consequently, political Utopias exclude or deprecate the idea of change. Plato assumed that even his perfect State would change—but it must inevitably decay into increasingly degenerate forms. (As Aristotle testily pointed out, "When it comes to tyrannies, Plato stops: he never explains whether they do, or do not, change, nor, if they do, why they do so, or into what constitution they change.") Karl Marx turned Plato around. Marx portrayed the whole of history as ceaseless and ineluctable change. Yet once the final state of communism was reached, all the historical forces that had hitherto made for change were, presumably, to vanish. Even democrats sometimes imply that democracy is a final stage in man's political evolution.

Yet in the entire history of political institutions, no political system has ever been immutable.

DIFFERENCES IN POLITICAL SYSTEMS

The fact that there are regularities among political systems hints that there are limits to change. That political systems differ argues that there are opportunities for change. If the similarities constrain us in what we can do, the differences enlarge the boundaries of what we may reasonably hope to do. Just as an awareness of the regularities may be both depressing and reassuring, so an awareness of the differences may engender hopes—and fears—about politics.

Yet if we have to live in some kind of political system, we do not all have to live in the same kind. It is the real or presumed differences in systems that make one precious, another tolerable, a third hateful.

As with people, so with political systems: differences are beyond our capacity to enumerate. Political systems have different proportions of people within their boundaries who are red-haired, green-eyed, over five feet tall, under twenty-four hours or over ninety years old, or whose last names begin with the sound "zee."

On Inundation by Data. If all facts are treated equally, we shall soon be inundated by data. For many centuries, information relating to political systems was not only selective but also scarce and impressionistic. Aristotle's feat of collecting information on the "constitutions" or political life of 158 Greek city-states was unique; and even that information was soon lost to posterity. Yet after centuries of wholly inadequate data, literally in the last few years the amount of information about different political systems has begun to rise at a staggering rate.

The rapidly increased salience of all parts of the world since the

Second World War, the growth in global communications, the diffusion throughout the world of political science and other social sciences as fields of active study, the development of data archives, and the increasing demand by political scientists for better data have all contributed to an information explosion in the study of politics.

During the 1960s, for example, whole new collections of data were made available on national political systems, to say nothing of the plethora of studies of subnational and international systems. These included handbooks of quantitative data,[1] classification of countries based on both quantitative and qualitative indicators,[2] analyses of specific problems using data on fifty to a hundred countries,[3] analyses of the results of opinion surveys among a smaller number of countries,[4] and in-depth comparative studies of national political systems or components of national political systems, such as political parties or political cultures.[5]

Although this flood of information gives rise to formidable problems of data analysis, it also opens up new and barely exploited opportunities for increasing our understanding of the similarities and differences among political systems, explaining how these come about, and determining their consequences.[6] Considered in this light, modern political analysis is poised at the threshold of a new stage of knowledge.

The Flood of Typologies. The information explosion also has been accompanied by a flood of "typologies," or proposed ways of classifying political systems. In fact, "typology" became such an "in" word among political scientists in the 1960s that it crowded out older but equally usable terms like "classification" or "classification-scheme." At the Sev-

[1]Quantative data on nearly 150 variables for 136 countries can be found in Charles Lewis Taylor and Michael C. Hudson, *World Handbook of Political and Social Indicators*, 2nd ed. (New Haven: Yale University Press, 1972.)

[2]Classification of 115 countries based on both quantitative and qualitative data can be found in Arthur S. Banks and Robert B. Textor, *A Cross-Polity* Survey (Cambridge, Mass.: The M.I.T. Press, 1963).

[3]See, for example, the analysis of the interaction of political, social, and economic factors in 74 countries that were "underdeveloped" as of 1950, in Irma Adelman and Cynthia Taft Morris, *Society, Politics, and Economic Development* (Baltimore: Johns Hopkins Press, 1967).

[4]The pioneering work is Gabriel A. Almond and Sydney Verba, *The Civic Culture* (Princeton, N.J.: Princeton University Press, 1963), which compares attitudes in the United States, Britain, Germany, Italy, and Mexico. For another example, see Hadley Cantril, *The Pattern of Human Concerns* (New Brunswick: Rutgers University Press, 1965), based on a special survey of 13 countries.

[5]Notably the seven-volume series on Political Development sponsored by the Committee on Comparative Politics of the Social Science Research Council, and published by the Princeton University Press. For example, the sixth volume, edited by Joseph LaPalombara and Myron Weiner, *Political Parties and Political Development* (1966), contains essays on party systems in most regions of the world except the one-party communist areas.

[6]See Richard L. Merritt and Stein Rokkan, eds., *Comparing Nations: The Use of Quantitative Data in Cross-National Research* (New Haven: Yale University Press, 1966).

Table 1   Aristotle's Classification

Rulers Rule in Interest of:

No. Citizens Entitled to Rule	All	Themselves
One	Kingship (monarchy)	Tyranny
Few	Aristocracy	Oligarchy
Many	Polity	Democracy

enth World Congress of the International Political Science Association in 1967, entire sessions were devoted to the topic "Typologies of Political Systems."

Schemes for classifying political systems are, of course, as old as the study of politics itself. Aristotle, for example, produced a classification based on two criteria: the relative number of citizens entitled to rule, whether one, few, or many; and whether the rulers governed in "the common interest" or in their own selfish interests.[7] This famous sixfold classification (Table 1) has influenced thinking ever since. But a half-century ago, Max Weber offered a classification that has had more influence among later social scientists than Aristotle's. Weber restricted his attention to systems in which the government was accepted as legitimate, and he suggested that the leaders of a political system might claim legitimacy for their rule, and members might accept their claims, on three grounds:

(1) *Tradition:* Legitimacy rests "on an established belief in the sanctity of immemorial traditions" and on the need to obey leaders who exercise the authority according to the traditions. Weber held that this was "the most universal and primitive case" of authority.

(2) *Exceptional Personal Qualities:* Legitimacy is based on "devotion to the specific and exceptional sanctity, heroism, or exemplary character of an individual person" and the moral or political order he has revealed or ordained.

(3) *Legality:* Legitimacy rests on a belief that power is wielded in a way that is legal; the constitutional rules, the laws, and the powers of officials are accepted as binding because they are legal; what is done legally is regarded as legitimate.[8]

---

[7]Ernest Barker, ed., *The Politics of Aristotle* (Oxford: Oxford University Press, 1952), Book 3, Chapters Six and Eight, esp. pp. 110–114. Notice, however, that Aristotle later reveals a more complex scheme by equating oligarchy with rule by the rich and democracy with rule by the poor. See p. 116.

[8]Max Weber, *The Theory of Social and Economic Organization,* trans. A. M. Henderson and Talcott Parsons (New York: Oxford University Press, 1947), p. 328.

To each of these three main grounds for legitimacy, then, there corresponds a "pure" form of authority: (1) traditional authority, (2) charismatic authority (from a Greek word used by early Christians meaning "the gift of grace"), and (3) legal authority. Weber recognized that these pure forms were abstractions or, as he called them, "ideal types." In an actual political system one might encounter all three kinds of legitimate authority.

Weber's and Aristotle's schemes have been all but pushed aside by the typologies that have crowded into political analysis in recent years.[9] Scholars have suggested that political systems can be fruitfully classified as autocratic, republican, or totalitarian;[10] as mobilization, theocratic, bureaucratic, or reconciliation systems;[11] as modernizing, totalitarian, traditional, and traditionalistic oligarchies plus tutelary and political democracies;[12] as Anglo-American, Continental European, pre-industrial or partially industrial, and totalitarian;[13] and as primitive political systems, patrimonial empires, nomad or conquest empires, city-states, feudal systems, centralized historical bureaucratic empires, and modern societies (democratic, autocratic, totalitarian, and "underdeveloped").[14] Two scholars who applied the statistical technique known as factor analysis to 68 characteristics of 115 countries "inductively derived" a typology of eight types of political systems.[15] One scholar swept conventional language into the trashcan by suggesting that political systems can be classified as fused, prismatic, or refracted.[16]

After the flood. *Is there one best typology?* Obviously, no. There are thousands of criteria for classifying political systems. Which ones we find most useful will depend on the aspects of politics in which we are most interested. A geographer might distinguish political systems according to the area they occupy, a demographer by the number of persons who are members, a lawyer according to their legal codes. A philosopher or

[9]Some of these, particularly those relevant to democratic systems, are summarized in Arend Lijphart, "Typologies of Democratic Systems," *Comparative Political Studies*, 1 (April 1968): 3–44.

[10]Bernard Crick, "The Elementary Types of Government," *Government and Opposition* 3 (Winter 1968): 3–20.

[11]David E. Apter, *Choice and the Politics of Allocation* (New Haven: Yale University Press, 1971), pp. 30ff. See also his "Why Political Systems Change," *Government and Opposition*, 3 (Autumn 1968): 411–417, and *The Politics of Modernization* (Chicago: University of Chicago Press, 1965), pp. 22–38.

[12]Edward Shils, "Political Development in the New States," *Comparative Studies in Society and History*, 2 (July 1960): 382–406.

[13]Gabriel A. Almond, "Comparative Political Systems," *Journal of Politics* 18 (August 1956): 391–409.

[14]S. N. Eisenstadt, *The Political Systems of Empires* (New York: Free Press, 1963), pp. 10–12.

[15]Phillip M. Gregg and Arthur S. Banks, "Dimensions of Political Systems: Factor Analysis of *A Cross Polity Survey*," *American Political Science Review* 59 (September 1965): 602–614.

[16]Fred W. Riggs, *The Ecology of Public Administration* (Bombay: Asia Publishing House, 1961), pp. 93–97.

theologian interested in distinguishing "the best" political system will use ethical or religious criteria. A social scientist interested in determining how revolution is related to economic conditions might classify systems by relative income and frequency of revolutions. Just as there is no one best way of classifying people, there is no single way of distinguishing and classifying political systems superior to others for all purposes.

Differences that make a difference. If there are innumerable differences between political systems, some are associated with such a broad range of important consequences—particularly consequences for popular government—that they are particularly worth stressing. These are: (1) paths to the present: (2) the socioeconomic "level" or degree of "modernity"; (3) distribution of political resources and skills; (4) bases of cleavage and cohesion; (5) the magnitude or severity of conflicts; and (6) institutions for sharing and exercising power.

Although in some degree these differences apply to political systems of all sorts, to focus the discussion let us assume our frame of reference is the political system of a country.

PATHS TO THE PRESENT

Every political system has had, in some respects, a unique past. This is more than an abstract point, for the inheritance of the past bears heavily on the present and influences the future. Differences in their past mean that all the 150 countries of the world do not have exactly the same options. A people that has known nothing but centuries of authoritarian rule is not likely to turn into a stable democracy in a week.

DEGREE OF "MODERNITY"

History leaves political systems embedded in societies that are at different stages of "development" or "modernization." These terms, now widely used among political scientists, have a parochial air about them, but their meaning can be made quite specific—enough so, indeed, to allow for measurement. There are, in short, profound differences from one country to another in the amount of income per capita, literacy, education, technical skills, technology, industrialization, urbanization, newspaper and magazine circulation, electronic communications, transportation facilities, and the like. These all tend to be intercorrelated: a country relatively low (less "developed") in one respect will very likely be relatively low in other respects, and the converse is true as well.[17] So much is this the case that Russett, using quantitative data, is able to classify the

---

[17]See Bruce M. Russett, et al., *World Handbook of Political and Social Indicators* (New Haven: Yale University Press, 1964).

Table 2   "Stages" of Economic and Political Development (107 countries)*

"Stage"	N=		GNP per Capita	% Urban	% Literate	Students in Higher Ed. per 100,000	Hospital Beds per Inhabitant	Radios per 1,000	% Voting	Central Gov't Rev. as % of GNP
I	11	Range:	45-64	0-18	3-48	5-63	.0001-.0031	1-63	0-55	7-26
		Mean:	56	6	13	27	.0004	12	30	17
II	15	Range:	70-105	0-19	1-68	4-251	.0001-.0056	3-78	0-83	9-23
		Mean:	87	10	24	86	.0006	20	49	13
III	31	Range:	108-239	6-72	3-91	3-976	.0003-.0056	7-161	0-95	9-37
		Mean:	173	21	42	165	.0014	57	41	22
IV	36	Range:	262-794	7-82	38-99	42-1192	.0005-.0143	37-348	0-100	10-40
		Mean:	445	34	77	386	.0041	158	69	25
V	14	Range:	836-2577	30-70	96-99	36-1983	.0077-.0125	215-948	28-92	17-40
		Mean:	1330	45	98	650	.0097	352	78	27

Source: Bruce M. Russett, Trends in World Politics (New York: Macmillan Co., 1965), Table 8.1, p. 127. Copyright © 1965 by Bruce M. Russett. Reprinted with the permission of The Macmillan Company.
* All data are for ca. 1960. GNP per capita is in 1957 U.S. dollars. Percentage urban is the percentage of the total population living in cities of over 20,000 inhabitants. Percentage voting is voters in national elections as a per cent of voting-age population. Central government revenue includes social security funds and public enterprises.

"societies" of 107 countries into the five major types listed below and described in Table 2:

Stage I. "Traditional Primitive" Societies
Stage II. "Traditional Civilizations"
Stage III. "Transitional" Societies
Stage IV. "Industrial Revolution" Societies
Stage V. "High Mass-Consumption" Societies

DISTRIBUTION OF POLITICAL RESOURCES AND SKILLS

Political resources and skills are distributed in different ways in different political systems. Although they are distributed unequally in all systems, the degree of inequality varies from one system to the next. For example, knowledge is a political resource that contributes to the formation of political skills. Access to knowledge through literacy and education is distributed unequally; but in some countries the inequality is greater than in others. At one extreme (Angola, Mauritania, Niger, and Mozambique) 97 percent or more of the population aged fifteen and over was illiterate in the mid-1960s. The median for 130 countries was 60 percent literacy. Among the lowest one-tenth of the countries, primary and secondary school pupils do not amount to more than 15 percent of the population between the ages of five and nineteen; among the highest tenth, the figure is over 90 percent.[18]

In all countries, only a minority of the population receives a higher education. But at one extreme, in a half-dozen African countries not more than 5 persons in every 100,000 are enrolled in institutions of higher education, compared, at the other extreme, with the United States (2840), New Zealand (2100) and the Soviet Union (1674). Even among the twenty countries with the largest GNP per capita there are great variations.[19]

Wealth is a political resource, and everywhere wealth is distributed unequally; but the degree of inequality varies. For example, the distribution of land, an important form of wealth in agricultural countries, is markedly unequal in all countries. But the inequality in landholdings is

[18]The data in this section are from Taylor and Hudson, *World Handbook*, Tables 4.3 and 4.5.

[19]*Ibid.*, Table 4.4 and 5.5. The figures overstate the differences, since in smaller or poorer countries unable to support institutions of higher education, some people are educated abroad.

considerably more extreme in Iraq, where half the total acreage is occupied by 0.7 percent of the farms, than in Denmark where half the acreage is taken up by 21 percent of the farms. (See Figure 6.)

The extent to which inequalities are correlated also varies from society to society. Suppose every person in a political system were ranked according to his relative standing with respect to the most important political resources in that society: let us say wealth, income, knowledge, popularity, control over communications, and command over police and military forces. If everyone's relative standing were the same, thus resulting in a perfect correlation, inequalities in resources would be completely cumulative. The more of one resource an individual had, the more he would have of the rest. If, however, an individual's standing on one ranking bore no relationship to his standing on other rankings (there is no correlation), inequalities in resources would be dispersed. Dispersion does not mean equality: in a system with completely dispersed inequalities, there could be inequality with respect to every political resource. Nonetheless, the difference between cumulative and dispersed inequali-

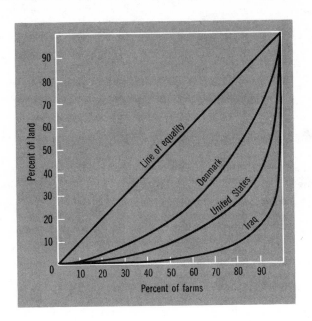

Figure 6   Lorenz curve of land distribution.

Source: Taylor and Hudson, *World Handbook,* Table 4.14, pp. 267-68.

ties is a crucial one, for in a society of dispersed inequalities, people lacking one resource might make up for it by having greater control over other resources.

Neither type exists in pure form. There is a strong tendency toward cumulative inequality, yet there appear to be significant differences in the inequalities among political systems. In countries still remaining in one of Russett's first three stages, inequalities are usually highly cumulative. In the industrial Revolution societies, however, wealth and income shift away from an older feudal aristocracy or landed oligarchy toward the new men of industry, banking, and commerce. Yet for the bulk of the population, in spite of rising incomes, inequalities are still strongly cumulative. (This is the stage that Marx witnessed in western Europe in the mid-nineteenth century.) In the later stages of industrialization, as incomes and mass-consumption continue to increase, there is a further diffusion of technology, literacy, education, affluence, and mass communication. This diffusion also may be accompanied by a marked expansion in interest-group organizations, political skills, and the suffrage. Even in these circumstances, inequalities in political resources still persist, but they become less cumulative and more dispersed. Hence it becomes increasingly difficult to identify a small, well-defined elite that "runs the country," for different elites tend to exercise influence over different scopes of activity and their relations become highly complex.

CLEAVAGE AND COHESION

The patterns of political disagreement, conflict, and coalition have different causes in different systems. This proposition and the following material should be read with caution: it opposes a widespread view that political conflict can be explained by a single source of cleavage, usually an economic characteristic like "class" or "property."

In spite of an enormous amount of speculation, theory, and research, our understanding of political conflict is still limited. Single-factor explanations simply do not stand up well against the data now available. The kinds of individual and group characteristics that are associated with political conflict in countries include not only differences in social status, economic class, income, wealth, and occupation, but also in education, ideology, religion, language, region, and family origins. This multiplicity of factors creates different patterns of political cleavage and cohesion from one country to another.

In the first place, history has left countries with different legacies of characteristics that foster cleavages and cohesiveness, such as language. Because of our experience, Americans may be accustomed to believing that other countries have only one language, which many do; yet our neighbor, Canada, has two. Or compare the Low Countries: the Netherlands has a single language, yet in neighboring Belgium a linguistic boundary has existed for over a thousand years that runs across modern Belgium and divides Walloons, who speak French, from Flemings who speak Flemish, a Germanic language. In Switzerland the boundary between the French- and German-speaking zones has barely changed since it first evolved in the fifth century A.D. On the other side of the world the Indians have over 15 major languages and 500 minor languages and dialects. In fact, in India many minority languages—English is one—are spoken by more people than there are in all of Sweden.[20]

In the second place, history has left varying memories of the past treatment of these differences. Take language again. The Swiss nation was built upon equality among its languages; as a result political conflicts and resentments caused by linguistic differences are nearly negligible. In Belgium, on the other hand, after a flourishing period of Flemish prosperity and pre-eminence (its brilliance is reflected in the great Flemish painters of the time) an economic and cultural decline led to the subordination of the Flemish to the Walloons, a condition that has embittered Belgian politics.

Finally, different stages of development tend to generate different forces stimulating cleavages and coalitions. In the nineteenth century, urbanization and industrialization in western European countries were accompanied by the misery and conflict that Marx was confident would finally polarize into a clear-cut conflict between an expanding urban proletariat and a decreasing capitalist bourgeoisie in which the proletariat was bound to win. Yet from the perspective of a later century, it appears that Marx was too hasty in extrapolating the early phases of industrialization into the indefinite future. Marx witnessed western Europe during the Industrial Revolution, Russett's Stage IV. He accurately foresaw that political conflicts would take place over demands for transforming the circumstances of the urban working classes. What he did not foresee was that long before the "bourgeoisie" was defeated in a conflict with the proletariat, three things would happen: the Industrial Revolution stage would begin to be transformed into the stage of High Mass-Consumption; the industrial proletariat would shrink in size and become an increasingly smaller minority of the total working force[21]; and because

---

[20]Something of the range of variation in the historical legacy of differences will be found in Marie R. Haug, "Social and Cultural Pluralism as a Concept in Social System Analysis," *American Journal of Sociology,* 73 (November 1967): 294–304. The author classifies 114 countries according to an Index of Pluralism designed to reflect the amount of heterogeneity in language, race, religion, sectionalism, and ethnic groups.

[21]It does not follow, however, that the working classes have become a minority. For a presentation of statistics to the contrary, see Andrew Levison, *The Working Class Majority* (New York: Coward, McCann & Geoghegan, 1974).

many demands put forward by spokesmen for the working classes would be met, the industrial proletariat, a minority, would become increasingly unresponsive to militant appeals for revolutionary change.

Yet in countries now passing through the stage of Industrial Revolution, conflicts over demands for ameliorating or transforming the situation of urban workers are likely to be a prominent feature of political life. Meanwhile, new social and ideological bases of conflict are emerging in the High Mass-Consumption societies.

THE SEVERITY OF CONFLICT

The severity of conflict varies over time within any given system and from one system to another during the same period of time. Whatever difficulties may lurk in this proposition must not be allowed to obscure the fact that on common sense grounds the proposition is hardly open to doubt. A little more than a century ago, Americans were engaged in killing one another on a massive scale in a civil war: that obviously was a severe conflict. The coup in Indonesia in 1966 in which the Sukarno regime was overturned and several hundred thousand people were killed was unquestionably a severe conflict. Armed rebellion, civil war, violent revolution, guerilla warfare, street battles, mass exile: these are conflicts of extreme severity. Speeches, debates, peaceful assembly, and peaceful elections are not.

Within any particular country, the temperature of political conflict fluctuates. Even the most stable countries are likely to have had a time of great turbulence and violence, a time of uprising, regicide, internal war—a "time of troubles." But the temperature of politics also fluctuates over short time-periods. If the Civil War marks the period of our most extreme conflict, there has been nonetheless a conflict of considerable severity about once a generation throughout our national history, beginning with the Alien and Sedition laws at the end of the first decade under our Constitution.

During any particular period of time, however, some countries are more peaceful than others in their internal politics. While some countries may be passing through their historic Time of Troubles, others are basking in a mood of reconciliation and unity. It is even plausible that national differences in culture and temperament may make people in some countries more prone than those in others to seek peaceful, consensual solutions to their disputes. However that may be, it is clear that in any particular decade, conflict is more severe in some countries than in others.

Naturally, it is not easy to design satisfactory measurements for a concept such as "severity of conflict," nor to gather and interpret the data. About four decades ago, a pioneering effort of this kind was carried out by a sociologist, Pitirim A. Sorokin. Despite the high level of his work, his findings have been largely neglected. Sorokin applied intelligently designed indicators of "disturbances" in French history from A.D. 526 to 1925, as well as to Ancient Greece, Ancient Rome, Byzantium, Germany and Austria, England, Italy, Spain, the Netherlands, Russia, Poland, and Europe as a whole. From his enormous and painstaking studies, Sorokin concluded:

> On the average in most countries studied, for every year with a significant social disturbance there have been only five years free from disturbances.
>
> It is not true that some nations are more orderly than others: all nations are orderly and disorderly, according to the times.
>
> While there are some differences among nations with respect to the violence and intensity of disturbances, these differences are neither great nor consistent.
>
> Only about 5 per cent of all the disturbances on record occurred without violence; about a fourth occurred with slight violence, however. The possibilities of a "bloodless revolution," it seems, are slight.
>
> Most disturbances last only a few weeks.
>
> The indicators show no continuous trend either toward bigger and better "orderly progress" or toward ever-increasing disorderliness.
>
> There is no association between internal disturbances and international war.
>
> Disturbances occur not only in periods of decay and decline of society but in periods of blossoming and healthy growth.
>
> What is crucial is the sociocultural network of values and relations: when the network is integrated and strong, disturbances are at a minimum.[22]

More recently, other social scientists have returned to this important topic. In 1969, in a report to the United States National Commission on the Causes and Prevention of Violence, a political scientist compared the amount of conflict in 114 countries. He found that between 1961 and 1965 the magnitude of civil strife varied from ravaging civil wars and extensive mass violence in countries like the Congo, Indonesia, and South Vietnam to a total absence of any record of civil conflict in such countries as Sweden, Romania, Norway, and Taiwan.[23] Comparisons with the United States during its turbulent years from 1963 to 1968 are shown in Table 3.

---

[22]Pitirim A. Sorokin, *Social and Cultural Dynamics,* vol. 3 (New York: American Book Co., 1937), Chapter Fourteen.

[23]Ted Robert Gurr, "A Comparative Study of Civil Strife," in Hugh Davis Graham and Ted Robert Gurr, *The History of Violence in America: A Report to the National Commission on the Causes and Prevention of Violence* (New York: Bantam Books, 1969), pp. 572–632. See also Ivo K. Feierabend, Rosalind L. Feierabend, and Betty A. Nesvold, "Social Change and Political Violence: Cross-National Patterns," pp. 632–687 of the same volume.

Table 3   Some General Characteristics of Civil Strife in the United States, 1963-1968, Compared with Strife in Other Nations, 1961-1965

	United States	17 Democratic European Nations	113 Countries
Pervasiveness: No. participants per 100,000 population	1,116	676	683
Rank of the U.S.		7th	27th
Intensity: Casualties from strife per 10 million population	477	121	20,100
Rank of the U.S.		3rd	53rd
Duration: Rank of the U.S.		1st	6th
Total Magnitude of Civil Strife:			
Rank of the U.S.		1st	24th
Rank of the U.S., 1961-1965		5th	41st

Source: Ted Robert Gurr, "A Comparative Study of Civil Strife," in Hugh Davis Graham and Ted Robert Gurr, *The History of Violence in America; A Report to the National Commission on the Causes and Prevention of Violence* (New York: Bantam Books, 1969), pp. 572–632, Table 17-2, p. 578, and Table 17-15, p. 628.

INSTITUTIONS FOR SHARING AND EXERCISING POWER

Finally, *political systems differ in their institutions for sharing and exercising power.* Many of us believe a corollary: that *political systems also differ in the distribution of power*—in the extent to which, in Aristotle's terms, power is distributed to one, few, or many. But given the problems in observing and measuring power discussed in Chapter Three, belief in this corollary must rest almost entirely on indirect evidence. And the most persuasive indirect evidence is the difference in institutions for sharing in the process of making policies enforced by the Government.

The processes by which governmental policies are made are exceedingly complex. Decisions of the Government seem to be reached as a result of some combination of direct or indirect participation by citizens, activists, and elites, acting through persuasion, threats, promises, direct manipulation, adaptation, deceit, and coercion. But the balance among these elements varies a great deal; the institutions unquestionably do.

They vary in two respects that are particularly crucial for sharing and exercising power. One of these is suffrage. This century has witnessed an all but worldwide acceptance of the belief that citizens of any country have the right to participate in governing that country by means of voting. Consequently only a half-dozen countries formally deny suffrage to their citizens today. Among the countries that grant suffrage, however, there are significant variations in the proportions of adults who are entitled to vote, and do in fact vote. In the United States, for example, because of legal exclusions, barriers, or inconveniences caused by residence and registration requirements and because of the legal, semilegal, and illegal exclusion of Blacks (practiced primarily in the South and now rapidly disappearing), the proportion of the population of voting age who vote in national elections is lower than in almost every other representative democracy in the world.[24]

Another important axis is the extent to which those who are closest to the actual making of a governmental decision must compete for the votes of the electorate in unrigged elections, in which those who oppose the conduct of the Government can compete on equal terms. Thus it is possible to distinguish countries, or other political systems, by the extent to which law, constitution, custom, and political practice protect freedom of expression, freedom to form and join organizations, access to alternative sources of information, free and fair elections, competition by political leaders for support and votes, and institutions for making government policies dependent on votes and other expressions of preference.

Because countries have differed and continue to differ along both these axes of the extent of suffrage and freedom of opposition, the world provides a vast array of political systems. At one extreme are the *closed hegemonies* that deny suffrage and suppress all opponents of the government. At the other extreme are the inclusive polyarchies that grant universal suffrage and protect the institutions listed just above.[25] Of the approximately 150 countries now independent, about two dozen are inclusive polyarchies and another half dozen might be called near-polyarchies. The rest range from repressive hegemonies that suppress every public expression of opposition to more tolerant mixed regimes with varying degrees of freedom for the opponents of the government.[26]

What are the conditions in which polarchies or popular governments are likely to be transformed into hegemonies? What are the conditions in which hegemonies are likely to be transformed into popular governments?

These questions direct attention to a problem that is not only one of the oldest in the study of politics, but also one of the most urgent and difficult in the contemporary world.

---

[24]Taylor and Hudson, *World Handbook,* Table 2.8, p. 55.

[25]Because the term "democracy" is used to label an unattained and perhaps unattainable ideal, to apply the term to existing systems invariably leads to confusion and controversy. Here and in later chapters I use the terms "popular government" and "polyarchy" (rule by the many) to refer to political systems with widespread suffrage and relatively effective protection for the freedoms and opportunities in the list above. Examples of polyarchies are the United States, Britain, Canada, the Scandinavian countries, Italy, and Japan.

[26]Typically, for example, even mixed regimes that tolerate considerable freedom of expression for critics and opponents do not permit the existence of organized opposition parties.

POLITICAL REGIMES: POPULAR AND HEGEMONIC

In Chapter Five we concluded that one similarity among political systems is that they all undergo change. Until the First World War a common view, particularly among Americans, was that history was on the side of democracy: gradually or by revolution, hegemonic regimes would be transformed into popular governments. The outcome of the first great revolution of the twentieth century, however, was not a polyarchy, but a hegemonic regime in Russia. In rapid succession the fledgling polyarchies gave way to Fascism in Italy, Nazism in Germany, and a military regime in Japan. After the Second World War, in most of the "Third World," hegemony, not polyarchy, became established.

What lies ahead for popular government? Is hegemony the wave of the future? Although our knowledge is too limited to justify an unqualified prediction, with some confidence we can specify a number of conditions that increase the chances of polyarchy. One can then make an informed guess where polyarchy is likely to exist in the future.

As we examine these conditions, it is important to remember that most regimes are neither polyarchies nor full hegemonies. If the flood of typologies described in the last chapter does nothing more, it should warn us against trying to classify all the mixed regimes in one specific category. However, we can usefully envision polyarchies and hegemonies as standing at a distance from each other with a number of regimes scattered between them. Ignoring inclusiveness, what serves to distinguish mixed regimes is that they are less tolerant of political oppositions than polyarchies but more tolerant of oppositions than hegemonies. The problem, then, is to determine the conditions likely to stimulate changes that move a country's regime toward polyarchy or toward hegemony. These conditions may reinforce the stability of an existing regime. For example, when conditions that favor polyarchy are present in countries with polyarchal regimes, then polyarchy is more likely to endure.

SOME DIFFERENCES THAT MAKE A DIFFERENCE

Let me call attention to several differences that are related to analysis in earlier chapters. Although an adequate evaluation of regimes must consider more than these differences, no satisfactory appraisal could ignore them. For they are among the differences that make a difference.

Differences in Forms of Influence

Autonomy vs. Control. Individuals and subsystems are more autonomous in relation to the Government of the State in polyarchies than in hegemonies. To be sure, this difference is partly true by definition. In effect, what we mean by a polyarchy is a system with a relatively higher tolerance for individual and organizational autonomy; by a hegemonic regime we mean a system with relatively lower subsystem autonomy. The rights to participate in and to oppose the government, the hallmark of polyarchy, require the State to tolerate and even protect autonomy both for individuals and for organizations.

As a consequence of these rights, organizations of untold variety tend to exist in polyarchies: private clubs, cultural organizations, pressure groups, political parties, trade unions, and so on. Many of these organizations actively seek to influence the government; many more can be mobilized when their members believe that crucial interests are threatened. By contrast, the development of autonomy threatens the nature of a hegemonic regime and the power of its leaders. Autonomous organizations are particularly dangerous. Hence in hegemonic regimes, organizations must be kept under the control of the government. Ultimately, in a hegemonic regime every individual and every organization is part of an all-embracing system of hierarchical contrasts. Although this limit is rarely reached in practice, it has sometimes been closely approached—for example, in the Soviet Union during the later period of Stalin's rule and in Germany under Hitler.

Persuasion vs. Coercion. In polyarchies, as opposed to hegemonies, political leaders rely more on persuasion and less on coercion.[1]

---

[1]Although he uses a different typology of political systems, David Apter presents a similar argument in *Choice and the Politics of Allocation* (New Haven: Yale University Press, 1971), pp. 32–33, and passim.

Some forms of coercion are by definition excluded or minimized in polyarchies. A regime that imprisons the leaders of opposition parties or suppresses critical newspapers, for example, is by definition not a polyarchy. Conversely, by definition a polyarchy must provide its people with rights to participate in choosing and opposing political leaders. An inclusive polyarchy extends these rights to almost all the adult population.

That these differences distinguish polyarchies from hegemonic regimes merely by definition does not make them less significant. Moreover, the difference in the balance of persuasion versus coercion is a practical consequence of the differences in the political institutions themselves. A group that has an effective right to participate in the choice of political leaders is less likely to be coerced in a conflict than a group without this right. This is most obvious if the group is numerous enough to constitute a majority. As long as the institutions of popular government are unimpaired, any attempt to coerce a majority of the population would be certain to fail, since a coerced majority could simply vote against the incumbents at the next election and replace them with more responsive officials. Because of this situation, politicians in polyarchies are rarely so foolhardy as to support laws directed against a majority of the people; if they ignore popular opinion, it is likely to cost them dearly. Of course, since laws rarely enjoy unanimous support, in any regime some persons could be coerced by laws that deprived them of some previous opportunity, privilege, or right. But even if people who participate in decisions sometimes suffer from the outcome, those who cannot participate at all are even more likely to suffer. It seems improbable that the Constitutional Convention would have permitted slavery in America if the black people in this country had possessed the same rights to political participation that white Americans had. In order to impose white supremacy on the recently liberated Negroes after the Civil War, southern Negroes were deprived of their newly acquired right to participate in politics.

In a polyarchy, it is usually difficult to coerce a large number of people, even if not a majority. For while extensive coercion places a strain on any political system, popular governments find it the most difficult. If civil disobedience on a grand scale, or even civil war, is to be avoided, a government engaged in coercing large minorities needs to have an imposing array of coercive forces at its disposal—a centralized and disciplined police system, a secret police, a compliant judiciary, military and bureaucratic establishments ready to obey the government when "duty" requires the coercion of large numbers of fellow citizens, and a body of law, constitutional doctrine, and practices that permit the government to employ these forces.

So imposing an array of coercion in the hands of the government would be a permanent temptation to unscrupulous leaders and a standing danger to all opposition. Although it is conceivable that a popular government might coerce a large fraction of the population on infrequent occasions and survive, the more frequently it did so, the more reduced the chances of popular government surviving would be. For example, when extensive coercion over Negroes was reestablished in the American South in the last quarter of the nineteenth century, in effect, the South developed a dual political system in which whites operated a quasi-polyarchy and black southerners lived under a repressive hegemony.

Reciprocal vs. Unilateral Control. Because effective rights to opposition and participation are diffused more widely in polyarchies than in hegemonies, individuals and groups enjoy more autonomy vis-à-vis the government, the opportunities for political leaders to employ coercion against their critics and opponents are more limited, persuasion is more readily available than coercion as a means of influence, and political leaders are more likely to be involved in networks of reciprocal influence. In polyarchies, government policies are likely to be settled by negotiation and bargaining. In hegemonic regimes, by contrast, the influence of leaders is more unilateral, and policies are more likely to be attained by hierarchy and command.

Differences in Levels of Conflict
Political Conflict vs. Civil Strife. It would seem reasonable to suppose that polyarchies would be subject to more conflict than hegemonies. In an important sense this is true: in polyarchies there is a great deal of overt political conflict. For example, opposing parties, factions, or candidates square off in an open attempt to defeat the other in a legislative body, in an election, or in the larger forum of public opinion. One might think that this high propensity for overt political conflict would push polyarchies into civil strife—that is, highly intensified, aggressive, polarized conflicts expressed in such forms as riots, sabotage, assassinations, coups d'etat, and civil or guerilla warfare.

Yet this is not the case. Although conflict is frequent in polyarchies, it occurs typically at a comparatively low level of intensity. As Table 4 shows, countries with lower levels of intensity in conflicts are predominantly polyarchies, while countries with higher levels are predominantly nonpolyarchies. As the authors of the study from which the data for table 4 are taken conclude:

> It appears that permissive countries are predominantly stable and nonviolent . . . ; however, the moment a modicum of coercion sets in, the situation

Table 4   Polyarchy and Level of Conflict (84 countries, 1948–1965)

	Level of Conflict[a]					
	Low					High
	1	2	3	4	5	6
Percent of total countries:						
Polyarchies[b] (N = 30)	100	77	60	23	9	0
Non-polyarchies (N = 54)	0	13	40	67	91	100
Total: (%)	100	100	100	100	100	100
Total: (N)	2	13	15	31	22	1
As percent:						
of all polyarchies[b]	7	33	30	23	7	0
of all non-polyarchies	0	6	12	44	37	1

Source: Ivo K. Feierabend with Rosalind L. Feierabend and Betty A. Nesvold, "The Comparative Study of Revolution and Violence," *Comparative Politics*, 5 (April 1973): 393.
[a] The authors refer to their scale as a measure of political instability. However, it is equally appropriate to describe it as a measure of the level of conflict, since "each successive scale point denotes a greater amount of political aggression and violence." For example, "dismissals or resignations of officeholders are assigned to scale position 1; peaceful demonstrations and strikes are ascribed scale position 2; riots and assassinations are at position 3; and large scale arrests and imprisonments, at position 4. Revolts are included in scale position 5, while guerilla and civil war and revolution are located at scale position 6." (p. 396)
[b] The classification of countries as polyarchies or nonpolyarchies is my own. No country was classified as a polyarchy unless it remained so throughout the whole period. However, see footnote 2.

is reversed. Moderate use of force seems to act as a stimulant to internal turmoil . . . Furthermore, it would seem that the pacifying effect of coercion takes hold only among extremely coercive regimes. . . . It seems that, at least in the global sense, coerciveness at first stimulates violence until a certain point is reached. Then coerciveness, in the form of tyranny, seems probably just as apt to bring internal peace as more violence. . . .

The obvious conclusion from this cross-national study of violence and coerciveness would indicate that political regimes that resort to force, especially if they use force inconsistently, must expect political instability and violence. On the other hand, the odds are overwhelmingly in favor of political stability for consistently permissive regimes.[2]

In countries with popular governments, then, overt political conflict tends to be frequent but comparatively peaceful. In nonpolyarchies, overt political conflict may be less frequent but it is also likely to be more

[2] *Ibid.*, p. 415. It is worth noting that the twenty-four countries classified by the authors as "permissive" were all polyarchies; of the twenty-three classified as coercive, none was a polyarchy; of the twenty-six classified as moderately coercive, only three (Chile, India, and Lebanon) were polyarchies. In all three, polyarchy was precarious. Chile subsequently fell to a severely repressive military dictatorship. In 1975, Lebanon was torn by acute internal violence. In mid-1975, the Indian prime minister, Indira Gandhi, proclaimed a state of national emergency under which she jailed hundreds of political opponents, including most of the leaders of the opposition parties, and imposed the harshest press censorship in India's history, even as a British colony.

intense and violent. In polyarchies, political conflict is typically terminated by negotiation, in nonpolyarchies by coercion. The characteristic mode of dealing with political conflict in polyarchies is by means of peaceful adjustment, while in nonpolyarchies it is by means of violence.

Differences in Institutions for Sharing and Exercising Power

How are we to account for the fact that in polyarchies, political conflicts tend to be handled by peaceful adjustment? As we know, some institutions are deliberately created to foster peaceful adjustment. The United Nations, for example, was intended to provide a forum for the peaceful adjustment of international conflicts. The countries of the European Common Market have developed institutions for settling many of their differences over economic questions. But for long centuries before these developed, an institution for encouraging consultation, negotiation, and the exploration of mutually beneficial solutions had already existed. This was the national parliament or legislature. The growth of a legislature, constitutionalism, and political parties has provided modern polyarchies with a complex network of procedures, traditions, rituals, and pressures involving elected representatives, spokesmen for interest groups, and experts, who mediate the conflicts among the manifold interest groups of modern society. It seems reasonable, then, that:

> The likelihood of peaceful adjustment to a conflict is increased in polyarchies by institutional arrangements that encourage consultation, negotiation, the exploration of alternatives, and the search for mutually beneficial solutions. Conversely, the prospects of violence are increased in non-polyarchies by institutional arrangements that severely inhibit such activities.

But may it not also be the case that the prospects for polyarchy are also better in countries where people settle their conflicts peacefully? Or are both polyarchy and peaceful adjustment products of the same causes —historical experiences, for example, or high levels of economic development? Although once again one must accept the unhappy fact that reliable knowledge about this crucial matter is fearfully limited, there is convincing evidence that the kinds of differences mentioned in the last chapter do influence the chances of both polyarchy and peaceful settlement. We have already discussed one of these, political institutions.[3] Let us turn now to some of the others.

[3]Limitations of space compel me to ignore a rapidly growing body of theory and data bearing on a key political institution, the system of political parties, and how it relates to cleavages, conflicts, and polyarchy. The reader may wish to consult Joseph LaPalombara and Myron Weiner, *Political Parties and Political Development* (Princeton, N.J.: Princeton University Press, 1966); Seymour Martin Lipset and Stein Rokkan, eds., *Party Systems and Voter Alignments:* Cross-National Perspectives (New York: Free Press, 1967); Erik Allardt and Stein Rokkan, eds., *Mass Politics* (New York: Free Press, 1970).

Paths to the Present. Because the path that each country has taken to the present is unique, every country has a different legacy of conditions bearing on the chances for polyarchy and peaceful adjustment. In a sense, much of the rest of this chapter is an attempt to find patterns of explanation in these richly different historical legacies.

Three variations are particularly noteworthy. Two of these—the legacy of subcultures and the treatment of the working classes—are elements in a larger set of explanatory factors that will be dealt with separately. A third is the historical process of change. In some countries, violent revolutions (particularly revolutionary wars for national independence) have helped to unite a people, while in other countries revolutions have left enduring cleavages. The American Revolution and the mass exodus of pro-British colonials that ensued helped to foster unifying myths and left few divisive scars among the American people. By contrast, the French Revolution left antagonisms that continued to embitter Frenchmen for many generations. Like the French Revolution, the American Civil War left enduring cleavages that are still apparent in American political life. In England, the Puritan Revolution led to civil war and failure; in contrast, the nonviolent Glorious Revolution of 1688 helped to foster the high state of consensus on constitutional matters that has been characteristic of Britain.

In a different perspective, some countries have enjoyed centuries of national independence in the course of which they have been able to accumulate political experience, develop their institutions, generate loyalties, break down cultural cleavages, establish a sense of nationhood, and work out ways of accommodation in their conflicts. Other countries

Table 5   Political Conflict and Level of Socioeconomic Development, 84 Countries, 1948-1965

| Level of Socioeconomic Development | Political Conflict[a] | | | |
	Low %	High %	Total %	(N)
Traditional	43	57	100	(23)
Transitional	32	68	100	(37)
Modern	83	17	100	(24)
Total: (N)	(42)	(42)		(84)

Source: Ivo K. Feierabend, Rosalind L. Feierabend, and Betty A. Nesvold, "Social Change and Political Violence; Cross-National Patterns," in Hugh Davis Graham and Ted Robert Gurr, *The History of Violence in America: A Report to the National Commission on the Causes and Prevention of Violence* (New York: Bantam Books, 1969), pp. 632-687, Table 18.3, p. 655.
[a] See footnote a for Table 4, p. 86.

have only recently become independent after decades or centuries of foreign rule and colonialism. These countries are new, still struggling to achieve a national identity, and still passing through the Time of Troubles. Racked by open or potential conflict, still unable, so their elites believe, to afford the luxury of polarchy, leaders rely heavily on coercion to keep the nation and its institutions intact.

"**Modernity**": **The Socioeconomic Level.** One of the most powerful influences on a political system is the "modernity" or socioeconomic "level" of a country. Thus a study of political conflict in eighty-four countries from 1948 to 1965 shows that relatively modern countries have a markedly lower level of conflict than countries with traditional societies or countries in transition from traditionalism to modernity (Table 5).[4] Not surprisingly, the transitional countries have the highest level of conflict. Therefore:

> Among the countries of the world, the chances for peaceful adjustment of political conflicts are higher, the greater the per capita Gross National Product and other indices of "modernization" associated with per capita GNP.

It is even less open to doubt that, statistically speaking, there is strong association between the socioeconomic level of different countries and the frequency of competitive politics in general and polyarchy in particular:

> Among the countries of the world, the frequency of competitive political systems and polyarchies is higher, the greater the per capita Gross National Product and other variables associated with per capita GNP.[5]

For example, in Russett's five "stages" of economic and political development (described in Chapter Six) 107 countries are initially ranked by GNP per capita, ranging from Nepal ($45) to the United States ($2577). It turns out that at Stage I (lowest GNP per capita) there are no polyarchies, while at Stage V (highest GNP per capita) every country is a polyarchy (Table 6).

[4]Ivo K. Feierabend, Rosalind L. Feierabend, and Betty A. Nesvold, "Social Change and Political Violence: Cross-National Patterns," in Hugh Davis Graham and Ted Robert Gurr, *The History of Violence in America* (New York: Bantam Books, 1969), pp. 632–687.
[5]A list of sources bearing on this point will be found on pp. 113–115.

Table 6   Distribution of 32 (Mixed) Polyarchies by Level of Socioeconomic Development[a] (1965)

	GNP per Capita[b]			Polyarchies		
	Total (N)	Range	Mean	Total (N)	Percent of Total	Percent of all Polyarchies
"Traditional primitive" societies	11	$45–64	$56	0[d]	0%	0%
"Traditional civilizations"	15	70–105	87	1[c]	6.7	3
"Transitional" societies	31	108–239	173	3[d]	9.7	9
"Industrial Revolution" societies	36	262–794	445	14	25.6	44
"High mass-consumption" societies	14	836–2577	1330	14	100	44
	107			32		100%

Source: Russett et al., *World Handbook*, p. 294.

[a] The classification of countries as polyarchies or nonpolyarchies is my own. Russett's five stages use six socioeconomic indicators and three political indicators (percent voting, percent military personnel, and expenditures of the central government). While relationships among the six socioeconomic indicators are strong, their relation to these particular "political" variables is quite weak, and the location of a country among the five "stages" seems to be independent of the three political indicators. Consequently, in spite of the slight contamination of "percent voting" with our measure of polyarchy, the relationship between polyarchy and the five "stages" given by Russett does not appear to be spurious.

[b] Calculated at 1957 prices.

[c] India.

[d] Ceylon, Turkey, and the Philippines.

Another example: Banks and Textor classify 115 countries according to their electoral system, as follows:

1. Competitive (no party ban, or ban on extremist or extraconstitutional parties only)   43
2. Partially competitive (one party with 85 per cent or more of legislative seats)   9
3. Noncompetitive (single-list voting or no elected opposition)   30
4. Ambiguous, unascertained, or unascertainable   33

If we compare the 43 countries that have competitive electoral systems with the 30 countries that have noncompetitive electoral systems, we find that competitive politics is associated with higher per capita GNP, greater urbanization, a smaller share of the population employed in agriculture, greater literacy, more newspaper circulation, and other indices of "modernization" (Table 7).

These and other data also support the following observations:

(1) In the vicinity of $200–250 GNP per capita and below, the chances of competitive politics appear to be so low that variations in per capita GNP do not matter.

(2) In the vicinity of $700–800 GNP per capita and above, the chances of competitive politics are so high that variations in per capita GNP do not seem to matter.

(3) However, the chances for competitive politics and polyarchy by no means depend entirely on socioeconomic levels, for there are too many exceptions and anomalies to be accounted for.[6]

The most dramatic deviant case is that of the United States. In the early nineteenth century, when polyarchy took root in the U.S., this country was extremely "underdeveloped" according to most of the indices currently used to compare socioeconomic levels. It has been estimated that in 1800, American GNP per capita was $231 (in 1965 prices)—that is, less than that of Guatemala ($281) or Nicaragua ($298) in the late 1960's. The population of the United States was overwhelmingly engaged in agriculture. Urbanization was extremely low—only about 6 per cent of Americans lived in places with 2500 or more people; and of course most of the other indices used to define the socioeconomic level of a country were equally "unfavorable." Yet in spite of these unfavorable indices, a polyarchy was successfully launched.

On the other hand, in the 1960s, the USSR, East Germany, and Czechoslovakia passed beyond the threshold of $700–800 GNP per capita, yet retained one-party hegemonic regimes. It has been estimated

Table 7   Political Competition and Socioeconomic Development (73 countries)

Percentages with:	Competitive Electoral System (43 polities)	Noncompetitive Electoral System (30 polities)
High degree of urbanization	82%	36%
Agricultural population over 66%	16	69
Agricultural population 33% or less	51	3
Per capita GNP $300 or over	67	30
Literacy rate 50% or more	79	48
Newspaper circulation 100 or more per 1,000 population	63	29

Source: Arthur S. Banks and Robert B. Textor, *A Cross-Polity Survey* (Cambridge, Mass.: The M.I.T. Press, 1963), characteristic 104.

[6]One of the deviant cases mentioned in earlier editions may, however, no longer be so deviant. In the 1960s India had a per capita GNP of about $100, yet was a polyarchy. In 1975, it appeared to be sliding into dictatorship.

that by 1965, per capita GNP in the Soviet Union reached $1657 (in 1965 American prices), or more than three times that of the United States in 1870.[7]

(4) Furthermore, evidence does not support the view that above the upper threshold of development, there is an ever-increasing "democratization," as this might be measured by a variety of possible indices of "democracy."[8] For example, over the past half-century the United States has enjoyed the highest GNP per capita in the world, but in comparison with other polyarchies it has also had one of the lowest rates of voter turn-out in national elections and one of the worst records for excluding and coercing a large minority.

Equality and Inequality: The Distribution of Political Resources. Political theorists have generally insisted that a high degree of social and economic equality is a prerequisite for a democracy. "Allow neither rich men nor beggars," Rousseau wrote in *The Social Contract.* "These two estates, which are naturally inseparable, are equally fatal to the common good; from the one come the friends of tyranny, and from the other tyrants. It is always between them that the public liberty is put up to auction; the one buys, and the other sells."

Existing popular governments fall considerably short of the democratic ideal, but even they would be threatened seriously by extreme inequalities in the distribution of political resources, for these would produce great differences in the potential coercive power of different citizens. If this general line of reasoning is correct, what are the consequences of different levels of socioeconomic development on the distribution of political resources, and hence on the chances of polyarchy?

The way in which political resources are distributed among the people of a country tends to vary with its level of socioeconomic development. With some important exceptions, inequalities in the distribution of political resources are greatest in countries with agrarian societies, less in industrial countries, and least in countries at the stage of high mass-consumption.

[7]Data on the U.S. population are from Bureau of the Census, *Historical Statistics of the United States* (Washington: Government Printing Office, 1969), p. 14. GNP data for the USA and USSR are from Angus Maddison, "Production, Emploi, Productivité," *Analyse et Prévision,* June 1968, p. 397. See also Charles Lewis Taylor and Michael Hudson, *World Handbook of Political and Social Indicators,* 2nd ed. (New Haven: Yale University Press, 1972) Table 5.5, p. 314.

[8]On this point, see Deane E. Neubauer, "Some Conditions of Democracy," *American Political Science Review,* 61 (December 1967): 1002–1009, and comments by Neubauer and Phillips Cutright in the same journal, 62 (June 1968): 578–581.

Let us examine this proposition in more detail by considering some of the characteristics of countries at different "stages" of socioeconomic development.

Countries at a very early stage of development usually lack even the rudimentary institutions required to sustain competitive politics. For example, such countries typically have a very high rate of illiteracy and lack the economic and social resources (such as supply of full-time teachers) needed to provide a formal elementary education for the young.

Countries below the lower threshold are overwhelmingly agrarian, and even above this threshold the economy and society reflect the predominance of the agricultural section.

Agricultural societies are particularly prone to cumulative inequalities, for the value of the land a man owns not only determines his total wealth and income but pretty much fixes his social status, educational opportunities, and his political, administrative, and military skills. Hence in an agricultural society, if the distribution of landed property is highly unequal, the distribution of all political resources and skills tends to be highly unequal; consequently, the distribution of power also tends to be highly unequal.[9] This is why a popular government is unlikely to exist in an agricultural society unless landed property is widely distributed with a considerable measure of equality. This point was first stressed explicitly by James Harrington, a seventeenth-century English writer whose ideas were accepted by many of the men at the American Constitutional Convention. Harrington wrote in *Oceana* (1656):

> Such as is the proportion or balance of dominion or property in land such is the nature of the empire.
>
> If one man can be sole landlord of a territory, or overbalance the people, for example, three parts in four, he is Grand Seignoir; . . . and his empire is absolute monarchy.
>
> If the few or a nobility, or nobility with clergy, be landlords, or overbalance the people to the like proportion . . . the empire is mixed monarchy.
>
> And if the whole people be landlords, or hold the lands so divided among them that no one man, or number of men, within the compass of the few or aristocracy, overbalance them, the empire . . . is a commonwealth.

[9]The causal arrow may run the other way. This is the argument of Gerhard Lenski in his spacious and well-buttressed analysis of the distribution of "power and privilege" in societies of various types: "Without exception, one finds pronounced differences in power, privilege, and honor associated with mature agrarian economies. . . . The very unequal distribution of power, privilege, and honor in them arises largely from the function of their political systems. To put it more plainly, in these societies, the institutions of government are the primary source of social inequality." *Power and Privilege* (New York: McGraw-Hill Book Company, 1966), p. 210.

In short, according to Harrington the distribution of power parallels the distribution of property (in land). One can witness this phenomenon today in many areas of the world that are predominantly agricultural. In a study of the relation of landholdings to politics in forty-seven countries, Russett found a marked correlation between inequality in land distribution and dictatorship or other forms of nonpolyarchy.[10]

Because polyarchies are heavily concentrated in countries beyond the agrarian stages, while nonpolyarchies are concentrated in countries predominantly agrarian, it is sometimes supposed that urban, industrial societies are more favorable to polyarchy than agricultural societies. Yet as the history of the United States and several other countries makes clear, an agrarian society is not per se inimical to polyarchy. Quite the contrary: an agrarian society that is pervaded by a considerable measure of equality can sustain the institutions of polyarchy, as the example of the United States demonstrates. But the circumstances that make for equality in an agrarian society are evidently rare.

Could the United States have developed and maintained institutions of popular government during the period when it was predominantly agricultural if it had not had its vast open frontier, which enabled nearly everyone who wished to do so to acquire land? Probably not. "The chief circumstance which has favored the United States," Alexis de Tocqueville wrote in 1835, "is the nature of the territory that the Americans inhabit. Their ancestors gave them the love of equality and of freedom; but God himself gave them the means of remaining equal and free, by placing them upon a boundless continent."[11]

As a country moves from earlier toward later stages of development, agriculture is displaced increasingly by commerce and industry. Although political resources become somewhat less cumulative and no longer so fully monopolized by a small elite, conflicts increase as hitherto dormant sectors of the population develop rising expectations and begin to demand more education, economic security, steady employment, social and economic equality, recognition, participation, democracy, and so forth. In short, as conditions favorable to competitive politics and polyarchy develop, so do the number and intensity of conflicts. Thus a competitive political system may begin to develop only to be swamped by conflicts it cannot handle.

Later, however, as a country becomes more fully industrialized, it develops an economic "surplus" well above subsistence needs that can be drawn on to facilitate peaceful adjustment of conflicts. Even if the

[10]Bruce M. Russett, "Inequality and Instability: The Relation of Land Tenure to Politics," *World Politics* 16 (April 1964): 442–454.

[11]Alexis de Tocqueville, *Democracy in America* 1 (New York: Vintage Books, 1955), p. 301.

number of conflicts remains high, their intensity declines as many of the older grievances are met, the most humiliating and aggravating inequalities are reduced, people come to expect that new conflicts probably will be settled by reasonably satisfactory compromises made possible by the "surplus," and political resources become so widely dispersed (though still unequally distributed) that few wholly defenseless groups remain.

To be sure, "subsistence" and "surplus" are not precise terms. What an Indian villager might regard as quite adequate for subsistence, an American would regard as totally inadequate. Nonetheless, common sense tells us that the average American middle-class family has a much greater "surplus" to dispose of than the family of a villager in India; likewise, the United States in toto has a greater "surplus" to dispose of than India does—which is one reason why we once provided foreign aid to the Indians rather than the other way around.

How does the existence of a "surplus" facilitate adjustment? Essentially by increasing the number of conflict situations to which there are mutually profitable solutions. A surplus makes it easier for parties in a conflict to be "bought off."[12] Conversely, violence and civil strife are likely to increase whenever a surplus declines or disappears. A surplus diminishes if the quantity of goods and services available declines (as in an economic depression); if the requirements for "subsistence" increase (as a result of changes in attitudes and ideas current in a society), or if both happen.[13] This helps to explain why many revolutions and other civil disturbances have followed times of rising prosperity, for during long periods when standards of living are rising, new expectations are created; the grinding poverty of the past is no longer acceptable. Hence when economic decline or stagnation encounters a rising curve of expectations, revolution or other forms of civil strife are likely to increase.[14]

Thus there appear to be two different ways of reducing cumulative inequalities and increasing the chances of popular government. One way, suggested by Harrington in England, Rousseau in France, and Jefferson

[12]For American experience on this point, see David Potter, *People of Plenty* (Chicago: University of Chicago Press, 1954), p. 122.

[13]In *Why Men Rebel* (Princeton, N.J.: Princeton University Press, 1970), Ted Robert Gurr puts the "intensity of relative deprivation" at the center of his explanation of "the potential for collective violence." Gurr distinguishes three different patterns of relative deprivation: "*decremental deprivation,* in which a group's value expectations remain relatively constant but value capabilities are perceived to decline; *aspirational deprivation,* in which capabilities remain relatively static while expectations increase or intensify; and *progressive deprivation,* in which there is substantial and simultaneous increase in expectations and decrease in capabilities." (p. 46).

[14]James C. Davies, "The J-Curve of Rising and Declining Satisfactions as a Cause of Some Great Revolutions and a Contained Rebellion," in Hugh Davis Graham and Ted Robert Gurr, *The History of Violence in America: A Report to the National Commission on the Causes and Prevention of Violence* (New York: Bantam Books, 1969), pp. 690–730.

in the United States, is by decreasing the degree of inequality in the distribution of political resources—for example, through land redistribution, tax reforms, and expansion of educational opportunities. Although many countries have moved in this direction, so far none has managed to eliminate sizable differences with respect to at least some key political resources, whether these are income, education, mass media, party membership, or others. The other way is by dispersing the inequalities that remain, so individuals or groups badly off with respect to some kinds of resources are better off with respect to others. This seems to be the pattern that exists in the United States and probably in a number of other mature industrialized nations. The two solutions are not, of course, mutually exclusive; a high stage of industrialization may tend to strengthen both patterns not only by decreasing the extreme inequalities that are mainly a legacy of early industrial systems superimposed on feudalism but also by dispersing the remaining advantages or handicaps to different groups.

However, even in high mass-consumption societies where inequalities are dispersed sufficiently to enable polyarchy to exist, the inequalities that persist are likely to be a source of discontent and of demands for greater democratization. As a result, new patterns of conflict may arise in countries at the high mass-consumption level. These new types of conflict, in fact, already have begun to emerge. The widespread involvement of university students in demonstrations, sit-ins, and strikes in the late 1960s may well herald the onset of this new stage. Just as advanced industrialization favors political democratization in the shape of polyarchy, the stage of high mass-consumption and beyond may encourage further efforts to democratize many institutions—political, social, economic, educational—in which inequalities persist.

Bases of Cleavage: Subcultures. As we have seen, countries differ in the extent to which the past has left a legacy of subcultural differences in religion, ethnic groupings, race, and language, and of memories of past treatment of these differences. Both aspects are important.

> The level of consensus in a country, and hence the chances of peaceful adjustment and polyarchy, are influenced both by the degree of subcultural diversity and by the way that differences in subcultures are dealt with.

A legacy of subcultural differences increases the area of potential conflict. The fact that New Zealand, Sweden, Norway, and Iceland are culturally quite homogeneous helps to account for their relatively low levels of conflict. Conversely, India's innumerable subcultures contribute heavily to her high level of conflict. It is not surprising, then, that polyarchies are much more common in homogeneous countries than in countries with numerous subculture cleavages (Table 8).

But the ways in which countries deal with their subcultural differences also help to explain levels of agreement and conflict. If the level of conflicts is higher in Belgium than in Switzerland, for example, much of the explanation can be found in the fact that Switzerland, with four language groups, two religions, and strong cantonal loyalties has managed to avoid serious discrimination among its subcultures; by contrast Belgium now suffers from several centuries of discrimination of Walloons against Flemings. The United States, while relatively successful in avoiding conflicts among a people marked by religious and ethnic diversity, has a record unequaled in any other polyarchy of discriminating against inhabitants of African origin, both as slaves and citizens. This legacy of discrimination is unquestionably a direct cause of the civil strife over the rights and opportunities of Afro-Americans that swept the United States in the 1960s.

THE NEXT STAGE?

In different countries, the various factors we have been examining interact in different ways. The interactions sometimes engender offsetting effects. More frequently, perhaps, they reinforce one another, and thereby dramatically raise or lower the chances for polyarchy and peaceful adjustment.

Looking over the analysis of this chapter, the reader may be tempted to believe that an inexorable historical evolution terminates in peaceful polyarchies. Reverting again to Russett's typology, everything seems to work against polyarchy and peaceful settlement of conflicts during the first three stages. For example, extreme cultural diversity, with all that differences in subcultures imply for coercion and conflict, is the typical lot of the "underdeveloped" country. Thus among forty-nine countries at a relatively low level of urbanization (that is, where less than

Table 8   Polyarchy and Subcultural Cleavages

| | Amount of Subcultural Cleavage | | | |
	Low	*Moderate*	*Marked*	*Extreme*
Total countries	26	28	27	33
No. of polyarchies	15	10	3	6
Polyarchies as percent of total	58%	36%	11%	18%

Note: The table is based on my classification of polyarchies and data on subcultural cleavages from Marie R. Haug, "Social and Cultural Pluralism as a Concept in Social System Analysis," *American Journal of Sociology*, 73 (November 1967): 294–304. In the table above, low is defined as 0 or 1 on Haug's index, moderate as 2 or 3, marked as 4 or 5, and extreme as 5, 6, or 7.

20 percent of the population live in cities over 20,000), over half fall into the last category in Table 8, indicating an extreme degree of pluralism. By contrast, among more urbanized countries, only about 12 percent have an extreme degree of social and cultural pluralism. Literacy rates show a similar relationship.

To look at the relationship the other way round, countries with an extreme degree of cultural pluralism are also relatively "under-developed." For example, three-fourths of the thirty-three countries classified as having an "extreme" degree of cultural pluralism also have a per capita GNP under $150; among twenty-six countries with a negligible degree of subcultural pluralism only one has such a low GNP. Or again: 70 percent of the countries with extreme pluralism gained independence after 1945, whereas 72 percent of the countries with negligible pluralism gained independence before 1914.[15]

Countries at the Industrial Revolution stage are, as we have seen, subject to conflict over demands for improving the lot of the expanding proletariat. Moreover, the way the grievances of manual workers, both urban and rural, are dealt with in the process of industrialization leaves a legacy of resentment or loyalties. In Italy and France, for example, the failure of governments to respond vigorously to working-class demands left a powerful residue of resentment toward the social, economic, and political orders. In New Zealand, Britain, Australia, Sweden, Norway, and Denmark vigorous and generous responses cemented the allegiance of manual workers to the prevailing institutions.

As countries approach the stage of mass-consumption, antagonisms seem to decline and areas of agreement increase. Some critics argue that what results is not so much a rational or spontaneous consensus as a manipulated or pseudoconsensus;[16] however that may be, there is impressive evidence that the process does take place.[17] Yet it would be hazardous to project this trend indefinitely into the future. Certain kinds of questions, such as foreign policy and the distribution of power, income, wealth, and other forms of privilege, do not lend themselves to technical solutions or to final answers. Around such questions, it is reasonable to think, new conflicts and new ideologies will emerge—may, indeed, have begun to emerge already—even in countries of greatest affluence.[18]

[15]Marie R. Haug, "Social and Cultural Pluralism as a Concept in Social System Analysis," *American Journal of Sociology,* 73 (November 1967): 294–304.

[16]Herbert Marcuse, *One Dimensional Man* (Boston: Beacon Press, 1964).

[17]Robert E. Lane, "The Politics of Consensus in an Age of Affluence," *American Political Science Review,* 59 (December 1965): 874–895.

[18]See Robert A. Dahl, ed., *Political Oppositions in Western Democracies* (New Haven: Yale University Press, 1966), pp. 398–401.

There is good reason to think that even when countries reach the stage of high mass-consumption, or whatever may prove to be the next stage as the twenty-first century approaches, politics by no means will disappear. There will be new cleavages, new ideologies (or old ones dressed in new clothes), and new conflicts. There can be no guarantee that these conflicts will be settled peacefully, that democratic ideals will be realized more fully, that new polyarchies will emerge, or even that existing polyarchies will survive. Yet it is not unreasonable to hope that as our knowledge about the central questions of this chapter increases, people will be able to act more wisely to reduce coercion, adjust their conflicts peacefully, and improve the performance of governments, as measured against the exacting and unachieved standards of democracy.

POLITICAL MAN

A starting point for all political theory is the fact that members of the human species live together. With few exceptions, human beings do not live in complete isolation. Whatever may be the elements of instinct, habit, necessity, or choice that induce people to form societies, man has demonstrated amply for thousands of years that he is a social animal. Yet, although man is a social animal, neither by instinct nor by learning is he necessarily a political animal—at least not in quite the same sense. Even though he lives in a society, he need not concern himself with the politics of that society, nor participate actively in political life, nor cherish the political institutions and values of his society. Some people do but many do not.

Nonetheless, because human beings are social, they develop political systems. Evidently they cannot dwell together without entering into relationships of influence; whenever these relationships become stable and repetitive, political systems exist.

In this looser sense, then, one might say (with Aristotle) that man *is* a political animal. Whatever his values and concerns, man is inevitably enmeshed in political systems—whether or not he likes or even notices the fact.

However, the individuals who find themselves within the boundaries of a political system are by no means equally concerned with political life. Some people are indifferent to politics; others are more deeply involved. Even among those who are heavily involved in politics, only

100

some actively seek power. And among the power-seekers, some gain more power than others. These four groups—the apolitical stratum, the political stratum, the power-seekers, and the powerful—are shown in Figure 7.

THE APOLITICAL STRATUM

Since the apolitical stratum shades off imperceptibly into the political stratum, an exact boundary between the two must be arbitrary. Nonetheless, they are, as we shall see, distinguishable.

Because many of us take it for granted that man is naturally a political animal, the existence of active and involved citizens, who make up the political stratum, hardly seems to need an explanation. What is more puzzling is the presence of an apolitical stratum.

It appears to be true, nonetheless, that in most political systems those who show great interest in political matters, are concerned and informed about politics, and are active in public affairs, do not make up a large proportion of adults; usually, it appears, they are a minority. Even

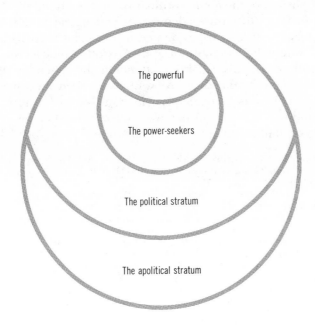

The powerful

The power-seekers

The political stratum

The apolitical stratum

Figure 7

in countries with popular governments where opportunities for political involvement are extensive, the political stratum by no means includes all the citizens. On the contrary, in all polyarchies, it seems, a sizable number of citizens are apathetic about politics and relatively inactive: in short, they are apolitical.

To be sure, there are significant variations from one system to another and from time to time. Yet the failure of a considerable body of citizens to take advantage of opportunities to participate in political life seems to be a nearly universal phenomenon. Even the Greek city-states, which are sometimes held up as models of democratic participation, were not immune. In Athens, for example (where the majority of adults— females, foreigners, and slaves,—were excluded from participation), the male citizens who made up the *demos* evently included a sizable apolitical stratum. If one compares the conjecture of a number of scholars that the demos in the fifth century B.C. consisted of around thirty to forty thousand persons with the estimate that there were only eighteen thousand seats on the Pnyx, where the Assembly of all citizens met, and the fact that a quorum for some purposes was six thousand, then it seems obvious that a large proportion of the demos ordinarily did not attend the Assembly meetings. In fact, "to ensure adequate attendance at a dull Assembly meeting, police with long ropes dipped in wet paint herded citizens to Pnyx Hill," where the Assembly met.[1] By Aristotle's time a century later, citizens received 6 obols a day for attending the Assembly, the town meeting of Athens.[2] Sometimes New England town meetings are regarded as models of democratic participation. But just as in Athens, in New England towns many citizens were unconcerned about exercising their rights or fulfilling their political obligations.[3] Even today the prob-

[1]C. M. Bowra, *Classical Greece* (New York: Time, 1965), p. 108. The figures in the preceding sentence are from Bowra, on the page cited, and H. D. F. Kitto, *The Greeks* (Baltimore: Penguin Books, 1951, 1957), p. 131.

[2]Aristotle, *On the Constitution of Athens,* Appendix IV in Ernest Barker, ed., *The Politics of Aristotle* (New York: Oxford University Press, 1962), pp. 379–383.

[3]In New Haven, for example, the problem seems to have been a persistent one. In 1642 the General Court of the Colony "voted that any freeman who after due warning, should fail to appear in the General Courts before the Secretary finished the roll-call, should be fined 1s, 6d; and that any of the rest of the planters who should be absent after their names were read, should be fined one shilling. The novelty of the first few years had worn away, and attendance at the General Courts seemed, to many, burdensome." A century later the problem was still unsolved in New Haven. In 1784 the old colonial town officially became a city, and the first city elections were held. Of some 600 males living in the city, about 250 were excluded as voters either because they could not meet the property requirements or because they had been loyal to Great Britain. Of the 343 eligible males, about one-fourth failed to take the oath and hence could not vote in the first election. Although most of those who were qualified to vote did actually vote for the mayoralty candidates, two days later only about a hundred citizens (out of 261 eligible) showed up to vote for the councilmen. Charles / H. Levermore, *The Republic of New Haven* (Baltimore: Johns Hopkins University Press, 1886), pp. 44, 231

lem is acute. In most polyarchies, between a fifth and a third of the eligible voters usually do not vote in national elections, and much larger fractions abstain from other kinds of political activity. Only about half the adults in the United States and Germany, and still fewer in Britain, France, Italy, and Mexico, follow public affairs in newspapers or on the radio or television.[4]

Why is it that even in modern societies with widespread education, universal suffrage, and democratic political systems the apolitical stratum is so large? To answer this question would require much more space than can be given here, but a short if somewhat formal answer can be given.[5] There seem to be several fundamental reasons why people do not become involved in politics.

(1) *You are less likely to get involved in politics if you place a low value on the rewards expected from political involvement relative to the rewards you expect from other kinds of activity.* The rewards a person may gain (or expect) from political activity can be conveniently divided into two kinds: *direct gratifications* received from the activity itself and *instrumental benefits* brought about as a consequence of the activity.

Direct gratifications from political involvement include the sense of fulfilling one's obligations as a citizen, the pleasures of social interaction with friends and acquaintances, heightened self-esteem from contact with important persons or access to inside information, the excitement of politics as a game or contest in which one's side may win or lose, and so on. For many people, however, political activity is a good deal less gratifying than other outlets—for example, family, recreation, friendships formed at work or in one's neighborhood. For many, political involvement yields far less affection, income, security, respect, excitement, and other values than working at one's job, watching television, reading, fishing, playing with the children, attending a football game, or assembling a new hi-fi set. The explanation, no doubt, lies in the fact that man is not by instinct a reasonable, reasoning, civic-minded being. Many of our most imperious desires and the source of many of our most powerful gratifications can be traced to ancient and persistent biological and physiological drives, needs, and wants. Organized political life arrived late in man's evolution; today man learns how to behave as a political participant

[4]Gabriel A. Almond and Sidney Verba, *The Civic Culture* (Boston: Little, Brown and Company, 1965), Table II.5, p. 56, and Philip E. Converse and Georges Dupeux, "Politicization of the Electorate in France and the United States," in Angus Campbell, Philip E. Converse, Warren E. Miller, and Donald E. Stokes, *Elections and the Political Order* (New York: John Wiley and Sons, 1966), pp. 269–291.

[5]A much more complete analysis can be found in the comprehensive study of participation in the United States by Sidney Verba and Norman H. Nie, *Participation in America: Political Democracy and Social Equality* (New York: Harper & Row, 1972).

with the aid, and often with the hindrance, of instinctive equipment that is the product of a long development. To avoid pain, discomfort, and hunger, to satisfy drives for sexual gratification, love, security, and respect are insistent and primordial needs. The means of satisfying them quickly and concretely generally lie outside political life.

Instrumental benefits expected from political activity may be divided roughly into two kinds. Some are special benefits for the particular person or his family—a job from party leaders, or pay for being a pollwatcher, graft, and so on. Or the benefits may be favorable government decisions: "the government issues a zoning variance to an individual so that he can enlarge his home, provides a license, grants an exemption from the army because of a family hardship, removes an unsightly telephone pole, offers agricultural assistance or agrees to provide a better water supply to a given home".[6] For some people, special benefits provide a sufficient incentive for political participation. The old-fashioned American political machine built the loyalty of its followers and party workers essentially on special benefits.

But particularized benefits rarely are extended widely enough to involve the whole citizen body. All that most citizens hope to gain from government are collective benefits (or costs)—consequences of decisions that affect a large category of persons such as tax payers, social security beneficiaries, automobile drivers, and so on. In decisions about war and peace, foreign affairs, military policy and a number of other matters, the collectivity may include virtually the whole citizen body. However, some people do not believe that they stand to benefit from these governmental activities. In a survey of political attitudes and activities of citizens in four polyarchies and one regime dominated by a single party (Mexico), about three-quarters of the people in the United States and Britain thought the activities of the national government tended to improve conditions in the area, about half thought the same in Germany and Italy, and a sixth in Mexico. The rest were in varying degrees hostile, doubtful, uncertain, or without an opinion.[7] For some persons, then, the rewards of political involvement are distant and vague, whereas the rewards of other activities are more immediate and concrete.

In short, for many people the opportunity costs of political involvement are simply too high to make it worthwhile. These people are unwill-

[6] *Ibid.*, p. 49. The distinction between the two forms of participation described in this and the following paragraph is taken from Verba's and Nie's discussion.
[7] Gabriel A. Almond and Sidney Verba, *The Civic Culture* (Boston: Little, Brown and Company, 1965), Table II.3, p. 48.

ing to forego immediate, certain, and concrete benefits or gratifications derived from nonpolitical activities to obtain the more remote, uncertain, and abstract benefits that might ensue from political participation.

(2) *You are less likely to get involved in politics if you think that there is no significant difference in the alternatives before you and, consequently, that what you do won't matter.* Thus people who say they don't care "which party wins the presidential election this fall" are much less likely to vote in American presidential elections than those who say they care a good deal.[8] Some people fail to vote or otherwise participate in politics because they believe the parties do not offer them a real choice. This view may be more common among Americans than among citizens of some other polyarchies. For example, in a comparison of Americans and Norwegians, among Americans "40 percent thought the two parties were about the same, and an additional 8 percent didn't know whether they differed or not." By contrast, among the Norwegians, only "11 percent felt that there were no differences between the parties; an additional 8 percent did not know whether there were differences or not"[9]

(3) *You are less likely to become involved in politics if you think that what you do won't matter because you can't significantly change the outcome anyway.* A great many surveys have demonstrated a strong relationship between the confidence that what one does really matters and the extent of one's political involvement. The weaker one's "sense of political efficacy," the less likely one is to become involved.[10]

The confidence one has in one's capacity to be effective in political life depends on many factors. Confidence may, of course, reflect a realistic appraisal of a situation. It is hardly surprising that people who see an up-coming election as a completely one-sided affair are less likely to vote than those who believe that it is going to be close. Even people who care a great deal about the outcome of an election may decide not to vote if they believe that the election is too one-sided for their vote to make any difference.[11] Nor should it be too surprising that in a number of coun-

---

[8]Angus Campbell, Philip E. Converse, Warren E. Miller, and Donald E. Stokes, *The American Voter* (New York: John Wiley & Sons, 1960), p. 104.

[9]Angus Campbell and Henry Valen, "Party Identification in Norway and the United States," in Campbell et al., *Elections and the Political Order* (New York, John Wiley & Sons, 1966), p. 258.

[10]Campbell et all, *The American Voter*, p. 105, and Robert R. Alford and Harry M. Scoble, "Sources of Local Political Involvement," *American Political Science Review* 62 (December 1968), pp. 1192–1206, at p. 1200.

[11]Campbell et al., *The American Voter*, Table 5.3, p. 99.

tries people are likely to have more confidence in their capacity to be effective in changing the conduct of government at the local level than at the national level.[12]

Whether the judgment is realistic or not, many citizens are weighed down by a sense that officials just won't pay attention "to people like me." In the United States, political self-confidence—the sense of political efficacy—tends to increase, the higher one's income, social standing, political experience, and, most of all, education.

Probably one's "personality" has some bearing on one's sense of efficacy. Optimism or pessimism about one's chances of influencing policy probably is related to deeper personality factors, such as an underlying sense of confidence that pervades a person's entire outlook[13] One's political confidence, or lack of it, may feed on itself. A person lacking in confidence may avoid politics, thus decreasing his chances of being effective and further diminishing his confidence. Conversely, a confident person may, as a result of his political involvement, grow even more confident.

(4) *You are less likely to become involved in politics if you believe that the outcome will be relatively satisfactory to you without your involvement.* A citizen who believes a particular political decision is important nevertheless might not become involved in it if he feels quite confident that the decision will turn out well anyway. Just as low confidence in one's political efficacy discourages participation, so too, high confidence in the all-round justice legitimacy, stability, and fairness of decisions in one's political system may make one's participation seem unnecessary.

(5) *You are less likely to get involved in politics if you feel that your knowledge is too limited for you to be effective.* In every country, it seems, large numbers of people feel they do not understand politics very well.[14] It is not surprising that some of them turn away from politics entirely.

(6) *Finally, the greater the obstacles placed in your way, the less likely you are to become involved in politics.* When a person expects high rewards from an activity, he is willing to overcome great obstacles and incur high "costs" to gain them. But when he believes the rewards are going to be low or nonexistent, even modest obstacles and costs are enough to discourage him. Why bother to climb over a fence if the grass is not greener on the other side?

---

[12]Robert A. Dahl and Edward R. Tufte, *Size and Democracy* (Stanford, Calif.: Stanford University Press, 1973), pp. 53–65.
[13]Campbell et al., *The American Voter*, pp. 516–519.
[14]Dahl and Tufte, *Size and Democracy*, Table 4.8, p. 54.

Thus there is good reason for thinking that the markedly low turn-out in national elections in the United States, as compared with almost all other countries, is caused partly by an additional barrier to voting—registration requirements. In other countries citizens do not have to "register" or may do so in a simple, convenient, almost automatic way. In the United States, differences in registration procedures and requirements tend to effect the percentage of the population of voting age that registers. Seemingly small matters make a difference; for example, according to one estimate, extending the closing date from one month before the election day to one week "would tend to increase the percentage of the population registered by about 3.6 per cent."[15]

The costs of political involvement also may vary with different activities. As Verba and Nie have emphasized, some activities, such as campaigning, involve conflict with other participants; people who dislike conflict, then, are more likely to stay away from these forms of participation. In addition, they point out, some activities—getting in touch with an official, for example—require a much more initiative than does voting.[16] It is hardly surprising that voting is far more common than citizen-initiated contacts with officials.

THE POLITICAL STRATUM

All the forces we have just examined also can work in reverse. It seems obvious that you are *more* likely to become involved in politics if you:

1. value the rewards to be gained
2. think the alternatives are important
3. are confident that you can help to change the outcome
4. believe the outcome will be unsatisfactory if you don't act
5. have knowledge or skill that bears on the question at hand
6. must overcome fewer obstacles to act.

Because of these and other factors, some people *are* interested in politics, *are* concerned and informed about politics, and *do* participate in political life. These people constitute the political stratum.

Yet the same forces seem to operate within the political stratum: some people are much more interested, concerned, informed, and active than others. In countries with popular governments where citizens are

[15]Stanley Kelley, Jr., Richard E. Ayers, and William G. Bowen, "Registration and Voting: Putting First Things First," *American Political Science Review* 61 (June 1967): 367.
[16]Verba and Nie, *Participation in America*, pp. 50–51.

Table 9   Percentage Who Say They Have Attempted to Influence the Government (by Country)

Country	Local Government[a]	National Legislature[b]	N
U.S.	28%	16%	970
U.K.	15	6	963
Germany	14	3	955
Italy	8	2	995
Mexico	6	3	1295

Source: Almond and Verba survey, unpublished data.
[a] "Have you ever done anything to try to influence a local decision?"
[b] "Have you ever done anything to try to influence an act of the [national legislature]?"

legally free to participate in a wide variety of political acts, the more demanding, the more time-consuming, costly, or difficult the activities are, the smaller are the numbers who engage in them. Citizens are much more likely to vote, for example, than to attend a political meeting, more likely to attend a meeting than to work actively for a candidate or party. Few citizens try to influence an act of the national legislature or, for that matter, the more accessible officials of the local government (see Table 9).[17] In the most complete study of political participation among Americans, (see Table 10), Verba and Nie have shown that "voting in Presidential elections is the only participatory act out of our rather extensive list of activities that is performed by a majority of those interviewed."[18]

In addition, however, Verba and Nie discovered a phenomenon that had been largely overlooked in previous studies of participation: there is a significant degree of specialization within the political stratum. They found that Americans could be divided into six types:

The Inactives (22 percent) who take "almost no part in political life." These are equivalent to our apolitical stratum.

The Voting Specialists (21 percent) who vote in Presidential elections but do little else. While this single activity distinguishes them from the inactives, the fact that they *only* vote also distinguishes them sharply from participants who do something *in addition* to voting.

[17]For example, for France, see Converse and Dupeux in *Readings in Modern Political Analysis*, p. 408. For Britian, see Richard Rose, *Politics in England* (Boston: Little, Brown and Co., 1964), p. 89. For a comparison of Norway and the United States, see S. Rokkan and A. Campbell, "Citizen Participation in Political Life: A Comparison of Data for Norway and the United States of America," in *Decisions and Decision-Makers in the Modern State*, J. Meynaud, ed. (Paris: UNESCO, 1967), pp. 254–255.
[18]Verba and Nie, *Participation in America*, p. 31.

Table 10   Percentage of Americans Engaging in Twelve Different Acts of Political Participation

Type of political participation	Percentage
1. Report regularly voting in Presidential elections	72
2. Report always voting in local elections	47
3. Active in a least one organization involved in community problems	32
4. Have worked with others in trying to solve some community problems	30
5. Have attempted to persuade others to vote as they were	28
6. Have ever actively worked for a party or candidates during an election	26
7. Have ever contacted a local government official about some issue or problem	20
8. Have attended at least one political meeting or rally in last three years	19
9. Have ever contacted a state or national government official about some issue or problem	18
10. Have ever formed a group or organization to attempt to solve some local community problem	14
11. Have ever given money to a party or candidate during an election campaign	13
12. Presently a member of a political club or organization	8

Source: Sidney Verba and Norman H. Nie, *Participation in America: Political Democracy and Social Equality* (New York: Harper & Row, 1972), Table 2-1, p. 31.

The Parochial Participants (4 percent) who not only vote but also make particularized contacts with government officials for *special* benefits. However, they engage in no other forms of participation.

The Communalists (20 percent) who not only vote but also engage in community action for *collective* benefits. The Communalists, however, do not engage in campaign activities.

The Campaigners (15 percent), "the mirror-image of the communalists. These citizens engage in almost no communal activity but are most active in political campaigns."

The Complete Activists (11 percent) who "engage in all types of activity with great frequency."[19]

Thus the members of the political stratum are far from a homogeneous lot. They differ enormously not only in the volume but also in the form of their participation in political life. While it is true that the complete activists are a comparatively small minority, the Verba and Nie findings do show that half of all American citizens engage in some kind of political activity in addition to voting. Altogether, the political stratum in the United States appears to consist of about three-quarters of the adult population.

[19] *Ibid.*, pp. 79–80.

THE POWER-SEEKERS

Within the political stratum, then, some persons seek power much more vigorously than others. And some persons gain much more power than others. In short, within the political stratum, there is a substratum of power-seekers and a substratum of powerful leaders.

You will notice that what we have just said is a restatement of two propositions set forth in Chapter Five as empirical characteristics of political systems:

1. Some members of the political system seek to gain influence over the policies, rules, and decisions enforced by the government.
2. Political influence is distributed unevenly among the members of a political system.

Now, to seek power and to gain power are by no means the same thing. Not only are some power-seekers unsuccessful in their efforts but some people who gain power may not actually seek it—they might acquire it, for example, by inheritance.

We have, then, two important questions: Why do some people seek power more actively than others? And why do some gain more power than others?

Socioeconomic Status

Socioeconomic status is associated with all three factors that help to account for differences in influence: inequalities in resources, differences in skills, and differences in incentives to use resources for gaining influence.[20] Therefore, it is not surprising that political activity tends to be greater among persons of higher socioeconomic status. In fact, Verba and Nie found that in the United States socioeconomic status accounts more than any other single factor for variations in levels of participation (Figure 8).

There is reason to think that socioeconomic status may be more highly related to participation in the United States than in many other polyarchies. Yet important as it is, even in the United States socioeconomic status accounts for only a rather small part of the variation in political activity.[21] Among persons of similar socioeconomic status and

---

[20]Cf. Chapter Three, p. 37.

[21]For some international comparisons, see Verva and Nie, *Participation in America*, Table 20–1, p. 340. They show correlations between participation and Socioeconomic status of .43 and .37 from two different studies. Socioeconomic status thus accounts for less than one-fifth the total variation—leaving 80 percent or more unaccounted for.

Figure 8   **Status composition at varying levels of participation.**

Source: Verba and Nie, *Participation in America,* Figure 8–3, p. 131.

similar amounts of political resources some engage far more actively than others in the search for influence over government. Why?

The answers to this question can be grouped into three categories.

(1) *Men seek power,* it is said, *in order to achieve the collective good.* They wish to protect the interests of all citizens, achieve justice for all, benefit the state, or provide for life, liberty, and the pursuit of happiness. This is the argument attributed to Socrates in Plato's *Republic:*

> So far as arts are concerned, then, no art ever studies or enjoins the interests of the superior or stronger party, but always that of the weaker over which it has authority.
> Thrasymachus assented to this at last, though he tried to put up a fight. I then went on:
> So the physician, as such, studies only the patient's interest, not his own . . . ; and the ship's captain . . . will study and enjoin the interests of his subordinates, not his own.
> He agreed reluctantly.

And so with government of any kind: no ruler, insofar as he is acting as ruler, will study or enjoin what is for his own interest. All that he says and does will be said and done with a view to what is good and proper for the subject for whom he practises his art.[22]

The difficulty with this debate between Socrates (or Plato) and Thrasymachus is that the two men are talking right past one another. This often happens in political controversy; each opponent vigorously flails on argument the other did not make, and thereby fails to meet head-on the precise point the other did make. In this case Socrates was making a *normative* argument, Thrasymachus an *empirical* one. Socrates met Thrasymachus' attempt to describe how rulers generally *do* act by indicating how good rulers *ought* to act.

Socrates and Plato knew perfectly well that rulers of states do not in fact always rule in the interests of their subjects. Indeed, to both Socrates and Plato the very meaning of a bad or perverted state was that the rulers did not seek the good of those over whom they ruled. Later on in the *Republic* Plato undertakes a description of the tyrant:

> In every one of us, even those who seem most respectable, there exists desires, terrible in their untamed lawlessness, which reveal themselves in dreams. . . . Thus, when nature or habit or both have combined the traits of drunkenness, lust, and lunacy, then you have the perfect specimen of the despotic man. . . . When the number of such criminals and their hangers-on increases and they become aware of their strength, then it is they who, helped by the folly of the common people, create the despot out of that one among their number whose soul is itself under the most tyrannical despotism.[23]

In sum, many political philosophers have argued that leaders *should* seek power in order to exercise authority for the good of all. But probably no student of politics has ever really argued that this is the only reason, or even the principal reason, why men *do* in fact seek power.

(2) *Men seek power*, it has been argued, *in conscious pursuit of their self-interest.* This was the argument of Thrasymachus that Socrates purported to attack. Thrasymachus had said (according to Plato):

---

[22] *The Republic of Plato,* translated with introduction and notes by F. M. Cornford (New York: Oxford University Press, 1945), pp. 23–24. The English translations of Plato's *Republic* often vary somewhat, but in the passages quoted here the differences are not significant. The student may wish to compare *the Dialogues of Plato,* translated by B. Jowett (New York: Random House, Inc., 1937), vol. 1, pp. 607–608; and *the Republic of Plato,* translated with notes and an interpretive essay by Allan Bloom (New York: Basic Books, 1968) pp. 20–21.

[23] *Ibid.,* pp. 297, 298, and 300.

What I say is that "just" or "right" means nothing but what is to the interest of the stronger party. . . . In every case the laws are made by the ruling party in its own interest; a democracy makes democratic laws, a despot autocratic ones, and so on. By making these laws they define as "right" for their subjects whatever is for their own interest, and they call anyone who breaks them a "wrongdoer" and punish him accordingly. This is what I mean: in all states alike "right" has the same meaning, namely what is for the interest of the party established in power, and that is the strongest.[24]

Thrasymachus may have represented an early Greek attempt to find naturalistic explanations for political behavior. Since nearly all we know of him comes from his enemy Plato, his argument in the *Republic* probably is somewhat distorted. Evidently Thrasymachus was trying to explain how it is that although rulers always proclaim that they are seeking justice, different rulers impose different ideas of justice on their states. To Thrasymachus the obvious explanation of the paradox was that each ruler was simply pursuing his own self-interest; "justice" as it was actually defined in the laws of each state was a mere ideological rationalization for the self-interest of the rulers. It is quite possible that Thrasymachus used his analysis to uphold traditional Athenian democratic institutions against subversion by supporters of oligarchy who insisted that they and they alone were concerned for the good of the state. Undoubtedly he also employed his analysis to undermine the appeal of Plato's elaborate defense of aristocracy, which Thrasymachus probably believed was no more than a brilliant rationalization for the antidemocratic ambitions of the oligarchical faction in Athens.[25]

Thrasymachus' hypothesis that men deliberately seek power for reasons of self-interest has been restated many times. Hobbes, for example, held that men were impelled by their passions and guided by their reason. Passion is the wind that fills the sails, reason the hand on the rudder. Man, to use another metaphor, is a chariot pulled by the wild horses of passion and steered by reason. Man's desires are insatiable, but reason dictates prudence. With the aid of his reason, man can discover the general rules or precepts that will enable him to improve his chances of gaining the ends his passions dictate. All men, then, seek power in order to satisfy their passions. But reason tells them *how* to seek power to reduce frustration, defeat, and the chances of violent death.

One difficulty with this hypothesis, as Plato rightly saw, is that the notion of "self-interest," which seems transparently obvious, is actually

[24] *Ibid.*, p. 18.
[25] On this point see Eric A. Havelock, *The Liberal Temper in Greek Politics* (New Haven: Yale University Press, 1957), p. 231 and *passim.*

very complex. What one views as his "self" depends on one's identifications, and evidently these vary a good deal. How one perceives the self is not wholly instinctive, it seems, but also a matter of social learning. Likewise, what one considers to be in the "interest" of the self is shaped by learning, experience, tradition, and culture. Consequently, to attribute an act to self-interest does not explain very much. As a distinguished modern psychologist has said:

> The self comprises all the precious things and persons who are relevant to an individual's life, so that the term selfish loses its original connotation, and the proposition that man is selfish resolves itself into the circular statement that people are concerned with the things they are concerned with.[26]

Jones's self-interest can mean his pursuit of advantages for himself alone. Or it can mean his attempt to obtain advantages of all kinds for himself and his family. The Jones family now becomes the "self," and its "interests" run from acquisitiveness to zoology. Or Jones's self-interest can mean his attempt to obtain advantages for larger strata with which he identifies—his neighborhood, region, class, religion, ethnic group, race, nation. Thus both the "self" with which Jones identifies and the range of ends he regards as in the "interests" of the self may be extremely narrow or very wide, depending on learning, experience, tradition, and culture. Anthropological studies testify to the fact that notions of self, interest, and self-interest vary widely among human beings.

A second objection to rational self-interest as an explanation is posed by post-Freudian psychology. Thrasymachus, Hobbes, Bentham, and Marx all interpreted the search for power as "rational" and conscious pursuit of self-interest. But Freud showed that the "desires, terrible in their untamed lawlessness" of which Socrates spoke do more than drive human beings into conflict with one another (as Hobbes argued); they also drive human beings into conflict with themselves. These inner conflicts, according to Freud, are fierce gales that often blow out the flickering light of reason. Reason, as Freud saw it, cannot always guide the chariot drawn by passion, for these violent steeds turn on one another and in their battle the reins of reason become entangled.

Freud discovered, analyzed, and stated what those keen students of human psychology, the great playwrights and novelists, had always known. But since Freud's day, several social scientists have attempted to develop systematic theories dealing with the search for power.

(3) *Men seek power*, some recent students of politics argued, *from*

---

[26]Gardner Murphy, "Social Motivation," in *Handbook of Social Psychology*, vol. 2, ed. G. Lindzey (Reading, Mass.: Addison-Wesley Publishing Co., 1954), p. 625.

unconscious motives. One of the most influential contemporary explanations of power seeking is that of Harold Lasswell. It can be summarized as follows: The power-seeker pursues power as a means of compensating for psychological deprivations suffered during childhood. Typical deprivations that engender power seeking are a lack of respect and affection at an early age. The self, then, suffers damage; the individual acquires a low estimate of himself. (The self usually includes more than the "primary ego," the "I" or "me"; it includes parents, wife, children, friends, countrymen, co-religionists, and others.) In childhood, adolescence, or perhaps later, the power-seeker learns to compensate for this low estimate of the worth of his "self" by pursuing power. He comes to believe that by acquiring power he can either make the self better, and hence more loved and respected, or he can change the attitudes of others about his "self." With power he will become important, loved, respected, admired. He hopes, then, to acquire through power relationships the affection and respect he failed to acquire in his family relationships. None of his behavior, of course, need be impelled by conscious, "rational" thought. On the contrary, a great deal of the motivation is likely to be unconscious. The power-seeker does not necessarily have much insight into why he seeks power; he rationalizes his power-seeking in terms acceptable to his conscious values and perhaps the prevailing ideology among those with whom he identifies. In comparison with other people, then, the power-seeker is a person who: (*a*) places a high value on gaining power; (*b*) demands power (and other values) for the self (the primary ego plus incorporated symbols of other egos); (*c*) has relatively high confidence that he can gain power; and (*d*) acquires at least a minimum proficiency in the skills of power.[27]

Lasswell's characterization of the power-seeker is, however, subject to a number of qualifications, some of which Lasswell himself has pointed out.

1. A power-seeker does not necessarily seek power in the Government; he may seek it in other institutions, such as business, the church, and the universities.
2. Extreme damage to one's self-esteem "may be beyond compensating," and may not produce a seeking for power but "resignation, withdrawal, and, in extreme cases, suicide."
3. A low sense of self-esteem may be sublimated in ways other than political activity. One might, for example, be drawn to the stage and seek to become an actor worshiped by his public.
4. A person who seeks power to compensate for his own sense of inadequacy may not be effective in *achieving* power, since he is likely to stimu-

---

[27]Harold D. Lasswell, *Power and Personality* (New York: W. W. Norton & Co., 1948), Chapter Three, "The Political Personality."

late too much dislike and distrust in others. "A person with a raging desire for power ... will constantly alienate his supporters, thereby making the achievement of power impossible for him."

5. Survey research shows, as we have seen, that feelings of self-confidence and personal effectiveness are highly related to political participation; yet it seems unlikely that persons who feel self-confident and effective would also have a low sense of self-esteem.

6. Power can serve many ends. Hence one may seek power from many different motives; the need to compensate for a damaged sense of personal worth is only one of these.[28]

Of the three explanations for seeking power that we have explored, none seems entirely satisfactory. However, our discussion does suggest several conclusions:

First, whatever the reasons may be, some people do seek power more intently than others.

Second, scientific knowledge about the personalities and motives of power-seekers is still scanty. Everyone agrees that some peole seek power more ardently than others, but authorities disagree over why they do.[29]

Third, depending on culture, society, economy, and political system, power (as Lasswell and many others have pointed out) can be used to acquire fame, reverence, security, respect, affection, wealth, and many other values. It is not suprising, then, that men should seek power; nor should we necessarily assume that power seeking is abnormal or pathological. In its instrumental character, power is like money. Some men invest more effort in gaining money than others do; they do not necessarily do so because they value money, as such, more highly than others but because they see money as an instrument to other goals.

Fourth, power seeking, like other behavior, no doubt is usually a compound of conscious and unconscious motives. Men who seek power may know some of the reasons why they do so; we can hardly expect them to know all the reasons.

[28]These qualifications have been made by Harold D. Lasswell, "A Note on Types of Political Personality," *The Journal of Social Issues*, 24 (July 1968): 81–91, p. 84; Arnold A Rogow and Harold D. Lasswell, *Power, Corruption and Rectitude* (Englewood Cliffs, N. J.: Prentice-Hall, 1963), p. 35; Robert Lane, *Political Life* (Glencoe, Ill.: Free Press, 1959); pp. 126–127; Rufus Browining, "The Interaction of Personality and Political System in Decisions to Run for Office" *The Journal of Social Issues*, 24 (July 1968): 93–109; and Alexander L. George, "Power as a Compensatory Value for Political Leaders," *The Journal of Social Issues*, 24 (July 1968): 29–49, at p. 49.

[29]The state of knowledge is best described in Fred I. Greenstein, *Personality and Politics* (New York: W. W. Norton & Co., 1975); in his chapter "Personality and Politics," in *The Handbook of Political Science*, vol 2, ed. Fred I. Greenstein and Nelson W. Polsby (Reading: Mass. : Addison-Wesley Publishing Co., 1975); and in the July 1968 issue of *The Journal of Social Issues*. The entire issue, under the editorship of Fred I. Greenstein, is devoted to Personality and Politics: Theoretical and Methodological Issues. See also Fred I. Greenstein and Michael Lerner, *Sourcebook for the Study of Personality and Politics* (Chicago: Markham, 1969).

Fifth, it seems unlikely that all power-seekers have substantially similar personalities. There are too many different reasons, conscious and unconscious, why one might want power, and too many variations in the costs and benefits of power from one political system to another and from one time to another. Undoubtedly both Caligula and Abraham Lincoln sought power. Yet it is highly implausible to suppose that Caligula and Lincoln had even approximately the same kind of personality.

THE POWERFUL

Not all power-seekers, we have said, gain power. Indeed, although it is probably uncommon, some men who do not seek to gain and wield power may nevertheless exercise it. Why do some people gain more power than others?

In principle, if one gains more power than another (over X, with respect to Y) then we may look to two possible sources of explanation—to differences in the amount of resources used and to differences in the skill or efficiency with which the resources are applied. Some people use more resources to gain power than others do. Some people use what resources they have more efficiently, more skillfully.

Why do some people use more resources? Presumably because they expect to "gain more" by doing so. I may "gain more" than you from a given action either because the action is "less costly" to me or because the outcome of the action is "more valuable" to me. If A has more resources than B—for example, wealth—then a given outlay is less costly for A than for B (all other things being equal) because A has to forgo fewer alternatives than B. Or, in the language of the economist, A's opportunity costs are lower.

A man of wealth and a good deal of leisure can devote sixty hours a week to nonpaying political activities at considerably lower opportunity cost than a man who has to work long hours to make a living. In short, if A has more resources than B, the opportunity costs of allocating a given amount of those resources to gaining power are less for A than for B; A can make the same outlays as B at less opportunity cost or more outlays at the same opportunity cost. In general, then, some people use more resources to gain power than others do because they have access to more resources. And, all other things being equal, it is reasonable to expect that people with more resources will gain more power. To this extent, then, differences in power and power-seeking are related to differences in objective circumstances.

However, "all other things" are not usually equal. Even if their resources were objectively identical, A might allocate a greater share of his resources in order to gain power if he placed a higher value on the results. Why might A place a higher value than B on the results of an outlay of resources to gain power?

1. Because A might expect different results from those that B expects
2. Because, though both expect the same results, A and B use different values or different scales to appraise the results
3. Because, though they expect the same results, A feels more confident about the outcome than B does

However, A's application of more resources may not result in more power (measured in any of the ways described in Chapter Three) if B has more skill than A. For a deft politician may accomplish more with little than a clumsy politician can accomplish with a great deal. Whey then do some people have more skill in politics than others?

This is a difficult question to answer. To try to do so would carry us beyond the limits of this book. In brief, however, there are three possible causes for a difference in skill between two persons, whatever the skill may be, whether walking a tightrope over the Niagara, playing the part of Mimi in *La Bohême*, or serving as majority leader in the United States Senate. These are: (1) genetic differences; (2) differences in oppor-

Figure 9

tunities to learn; and (3) differences in incentives to learn. The first two are differences in situation, the third a difference in motivation.

We began this section with the question—"Why do some people gain more power than others?" Our answer is summarized in Figure 9.

VARIETIES OF POLITICAL MAN

Our examination of power-seekers and the powerful points up the seemingly endless variety of human motivations, incentives, orientations, and even personalities at work in political life. Attempts to impose a degree of intellectual tidiness on this disorderly array of human types have sometimes been notable for their insight and brilliance, but so far they have met with scant success. In recent years, however, social scientists have emphasized five factors that help to account for the varieties of political man.

A particular person's orientations toward politics can be explained, to some degree, in the light of:

1. His personality or character
2. The general culture, or, more specifically, the political culture, which he shares with others in his tribe, village, city, country, or world region
3. His earliest political orientations and how he acquires them—that is, his *political socialization*
4. His own personal experiences and circumstances, his life situation
5. The particular situation he confronts, or believes he confronts, at a specific historical moment

A consideration of several varieties of political man will help one to see how these five factors interact.

Democratic Man and Despotic Man. Is it possible to specify a kind of personality or character that is especially suited—or unsuited—to the operation of popular government? Plato thought so; in *The Republic* he vividly sets out his description of "the oligarchic, democratic, and despotic characters" and offers explanations of how these come about.[30] In one form or another, Plato's general hypothesis has been affirmed many times—by Machiavelli, among others.[31]

Empirical information bearing on Plato's hypothesis is still lacking, despite a good deal of speculation that, at least in recent years, has been aided by the insights of modern psychiatry and psychoanalysis. Is there

[30]This discussion will be found in Cornford's translation, pp. 268 ff. For the democratic character, see pp. 280 ff.

[31]For example, in his *Discourses on the First Ten Books of Titus Livius,* First Book, Chapters sixteen, seventeen, and eighteen, in Nicoló Machiavelli, *The Prince and the Discourses* (New York: Random House, 1940), pp. 160–168.

a "democratic" personality?[32] After examining a substantial body of work on the subject, one scholar remarks that "Almost all the modern students of national character are convinced the answer to this question is in the affirmative. Systematic evidence for this faith is unfortunately lacking."[33] Nonetheless, among recent students of politics who deal with this question there is "an extraordinary degree of agreement about the values, attitudes, opinions, and traits of character" that help to maintain a popular system. The most important are attitudes toward one's self, toward others, toward authority, toward the community, and toward values:

1. *Toward self:* A belief in the worth and dignity of one's self
2. *Toward others:* A belief in the worth and dignity of others
3. *Toward authority:* A stress on personal autonomy and maintaining a certain distance from or even distrusting powerful authority; in contrast to the authoritarian, the absence of a need to dominate or submit
4. *Toward the community:* Openness, ready acceptance of differences, willingness to compromise and change
5. *Toward values:* A pursuit of many values rather than a single all-consuming goal, and a disposition to share rather than to hoard or monopolize[34]

Is there an antidemocratic or despotic personality? Since 1950 a good deal of important exploratory work has been carried out on the characteristics of a syndrome termed the "authoritarian personality." A person is said to have an authoritarian personality if he is rigidly conventional; submissive and uncritical toward authority; aggressive and punitive toward people who violate conventional values; opposed to subjective, imaginative, tender-minded ways of thinking about the world; preoccupied with power and toughness; cynical; concerned that wild and dangerous things are going on in the world; and particularly obsessed with sexual "goings-on."[35] Because of criticisms of the questionnaire

[32]An excellent summary and critique of the leading theories is contained in Paul M. Sniderman, *Personality and Democratic Politics* (Berkeley: University of California Press, 1975), Chapter Five, "Democratic Commitment and the Democratic Personality," pp. 164–222.

[33]Alex Inkeles, "National Character and Modern Political Systems," in Francis W. K. Hsu, *Psychology and Anthropology: Approaches to Culture and Personality* (Homewood, Ill.: Dorsey Press, 1961), pp. 172–208.

[34]This list is adapted in slightly modified form from a list of Inkeles, *ibid.* Inkeles in turn draws heavily on Lasswell, whose work on democratic character is the modern seminal source. Cf. particularly Lasswell's *Democratic Character* in *The Political Writings of Harold D. Lasswell* (Glencoe, Ill.: Free Press, 1951), pp. 465–525, and Fred I. Greenstein, "Harold D. Lasswell's Concept of Democratic Character," *Journal of Politics* 30 (August 1968): 696–709. See also Karl Mannheim, *Freedom, Power, and Democratic Planning* (New York: Oxford University Press, 1950), Chapter Nine, "The Pattern of Democratic Personality," pp. 228–245; and Robert Lane, "Notes on a Theory of Democratic Personality," in *Political Ideology* (New York: Free Press. 1962), pp. 401–412.

[35]W. Adorno, Else Frenkel-Brunswik, Daniel J. Levinson, and R. Nevitt Sanford, *The Authoritarian Personality* (New York: Harper & Row, 1950), p. 228.

used to tap these underlying attitudes—often called the F-scale—many scholars have been skeptical of studies describing the political behavior of people with authoritarian personalities. Some social scientists, however, have tried to improve upon the earlier work by developing new concepts and measures. Among the best known of these are several questionnaires developed by Milton Rokeach for identifying such characteristics as open-mindedness, dogmatism, and rigidity.[36]

There is ample evidence to confirm the common sense view that people do vary a good deal in authoritarianism, open-mindedness, dogmatism, rigidity, flexibility, and the like. Sometimes investigations have produced rather startling results: one study of Italian members of parliament, for example, found that communist deputies were very much less dogmatic, at least as measured by Rokeach's dogmatism-scale, than the deputies of any other party![37]

Yet the connection between personality and overt political actions remains complex, obscure, and apparently rather loose.[38] It is no doubt a reasonable hypothesis that a popular government would have great difficulty surviving in a population composed *mainly* of individuals with strongly "authoritarian personalities." But it is possible that political culture might significantly channel the outlets for a democratic or authoritarian personality. In a predominantly "democratic" culture, where democratic norms, institutions, and practices have a high degree of legitimacy, some individuals with "authoritarian personalities" may, conceivably, acquire an overlay of democratic beliefs and habits that help them function "democratically." Indeed, there is good reason for thinking that authoritarian or democratic orientations are very significantly shaped by culture and by processes of political socialization.[39] The authors of the five-nation study cited earlier in this chapter offer an impressive body of evidence for the conclusion that the political cultures of these five countries vary in significant ways, and that these differences have a bearing on the prospects of popular government.[40]

[36]Milton Rokeach, *The Open and Closed Mind* (New York: Basic Books, 1960).
[37]Gordon J. DiRenzo, *Personality, Power, and Politics* (Notre Dame: University of Notre Dame Press, 1967), pp. 123–124. Robert D. Putnam found that in Italy deputies on the Left "are considerably more open in their partisanship than those at the Right. There is also a tendency, especially marked in Italy, for politicians of the Left to be more favorable to the principle of compromise. Indeed, among Italian Communists the acceptability of compromise solutions to political problems has become almost dogma. For some the dogma is probably only verbal, but for others it is deeply felt." *The Beliefs of Politicians: Ideology, Conflict, and Democracy in Britian and Italy* (New Haven: Yale University Press, 1973), p. 61.
[38]The best statement is Fred I. Greenstein, "The Impact of Personality on Politics," in *Personality and Politics*, footnote 20.
[39]An excellant comparison of Britain and Italy will be found in Robert D. Putnam, *The Beliefs of Politicians, op. cit.*
[40]Almond and Verba, *The Civic Culture.*

Conceivably personality and character contribute less than political culture to the shaping of democratic—or despotic—man. This view is supported by a recent study of the relationship between self-esteem and democratic orientations. Among three large samples of Americans—one of them consisting of political activists—Paul Sniderman found that "there are indeed fundamental differences in psychological makeup between those who affirm the principles of democracy and those who fail to adhere as consistently to them. . . . The democrat is more likely to have high self-esteem and less likely to be hostile." However, Sniderman suggests that the linkage is less a matter of motivation than of social learning: persons with high self-esteem are more likely to learn the norms of their culture, in this case the democratic norms that tend to prevail in the American political culture. It does not follow necessarily that in a different culture high self-esteem would lead to the adoption of democratic norms. On the contrary Sniderman argues:

> The same psychological qualities that distinguish a democrat in the United States may well characterize a communist in Soviet Russia; for insofar as the linkage between personality and political ideology is a matter of social learning, then high self-esteem (and conceivably many other personality traits as well) ought to drive individuals towards accepting the norms of their political culture, whatever those may be.[41]

Agitator and Negotiator. Two other interesting varieties of political man are the *agitator* and the *negotiator.* The classic description of the personality of the political agitator was presented by Lasswell in 1930:

> The essential mark of the agitator is the high value which he places on the emotional response of the public. Whether he attacks or defends social institutions is a secondary matter. . . . The agitator easily infers that he who disagrees with him is in communion with the devil, and that opponents show bad faith or timidity. Agitators are notoriously contentious and undisciplined; many reforming ships are manned by mutineers. The agitator is willing to subordinate personal considerations to the superior claims of principle. Children may suffer while father and mother battle for "the cause." . . . The agitator sees "unworthy" motives where others see the just claims of friendship. . . . [He] trusts in mass appeals and general principles . . . live[s] to shout and write. . . . [Agitators] conjure away obstacles with the ritualistic repetition of principles. They become frustrated and confused in the tangled mass of technical detail upon which successful administration depends. . . . They glorify men of outspoken zeal, men who harry the dragons and stir the public conscience by exhortation, reiteration, and vituperation.

[41]Sniderman, *Personality and Democratic Politics,* pp. 220–221.

Lasswell describes Mr. A., a typical agitator whom he had studied in great detail:

> A leading characteristic as moralist, socialist, and pacifist has been his truculence in public. Mr. A. speaks rapidly, with great fervor and earnestness, and his discourse is studded with abusive epithets, sarcastic jibes, and cutting insinuations. He confesses that he has taken an unmistakable pleasure in "rubbing the fur the wrong way." He enjoyed nothing better than accepting an invitation to lecture on social and economic subjects before conservative audiences, and scandalizing them. . . .[42]

By contrast, the negotiator is a compromiser. If the agitator feels contempt for the "unprincipled" conduct of the negotiator, the negotiator is baffled by the intransigence of the agitator, who sacrifices immediate gains for abstract principles. The negotiator is more concerned with an acceptable solution to a conflict than a just or perfect solution.

In politics the negotiator is that widely despised figure, the pragmatic or even opportunistic politician. In the extreme case, the pragmatic politician and the agitator hold diametrically opposed views on the importance of current public opinion. The pragmatic politician wants to know what public opinion is; he does not much care what it ought to be. The agitator is interested in what public opinion is only in order to change it to what it ought to be. The pragmatic politician seeks only to respond to public opinion; the agitator tries to make public opinion respond to him. Wendell Phillips, himself a famous American agitator of the nineteenth century, made an eloquent if somewhat biased contrast between the agitator and the pragmatic politician:

> The reformer is careless of numbers, disregards popularity, and deals only with ideas, conscience, and common sense. He feels, with Copernicus, that as God waited long for an interpreter, so he can wait for his followers. He neither expects nor is overanxious for immediate success. The politician dwells in an everlasting NOW. His Motto is "Success"—his aim, votes. His object is not absolute right, but, like Solon's laws, as much right as the people will sanction. His office is not to instruct public opinion, but to represent it. Thus, in England, Cobden, the reformer, created sentiment, and Peel, the politician, stereotyped it into statutes.[43]

Because he takes current opinion as given, the pragmatic politician is the instrument of current majorities. Because he takes public opinion

[42]Harold Lasswell, *Psychopathology and Politics* (Chicago: University of Chicago Press, 1930), pp. 78–80.
[43]Quoted in Richard Hofstadter, *The American Political Tradition* (New York: Vintage Books; London; Jonathan Cape Ltd., 1954), p. 138–139.

as an object to be altered, the agitator helps create future majorities. Both run the fatal risk of being born out of their time. The pragmatic politician born out of his time is obedient to opinions today that lead inexorably to disaster tomorrow. Born out of his time, the agitator is merely ignored today and, worse yet, forgotten tomorrow.

Wendell Phillips is the prototype of the intelligent agitator, Abraham Lincoln of the principled politician. Phillips was "an agitator by profession" who "made of agitation an art and a science." He became an abolitionist in the 1830s; after the Civil War he attacked the conciliatory policies of President Johnson, supported Radical Republicans like Charles Sumner in Congress, demanded the redistribution of landed property in the South, and thus sought to reduce the power of the ex-slaveholders. He sympathized with the First Socialist International, was "a homespun Yankee" socialist, and supported women's rights. It is understandable that a Virginia newspaper once described him as "an infernal machine set to music."[44]

Although Phillips supported Lincoln during the Civil War, the two could hardly have been more different. Lincoln was surely one of the greatest of our pragmatic politicians. If it is hard to imagine Phillips as President, it is difficult to think of Lincoln other than as President. Yet before he entered the White House he had spent most of his mature life acquiring and practicing the arts of the pragmatic politician. At an early age, in Richard Hofstadter's words, he learned "the deliberate and responsible opportunism that was later so characteristic of his statecraft."

> The clue to much that is vital in Lincoln's thought and character lies in the fact that he was thoroughly and completely the politician, by preference and by training. It is difficult to think of any man of comparable stature whose life was so fully absorbed into his political being. Lincoln plunged into politics almost at the beginning of his adult life and was never occupied in any other career except for a brief period when an unfavorable turn in the political situation forced him back to his law practice. His life was one of caucuses and conventions, party circulars and speeches, requests, recommendations, stratagems, schemes, and ambitions. "It was the world of politics that he lived," wrote Herndon after his death. "Politics were his life, newspapers his food, and his great ambition his motive power."[45]

It is reasonable to think that popular governments would suffer badly if either the agitator or the negotiator were absent. Negotiators increase the chances for peaceful adjustment of conflicts. Yet short-run

---

[44]For these and other details of Phillips' life, see "Wendell Phillips: The Patrician as Agitator," Chapter Six in Hofstadter, *ibid.*
[45]*Ibid.*, pp. 95–97.

peaceful adjustments may take place without considering currently un-popular alternatives, or at the expense of groups who have no spokesmen and are inadequately represented. The agitator often focuses attention on these neglected alternatives or groups, and, paradoxical as it may seem, may thereby contribute to the discovery of better short-run and long-run solutions. This was Wendell Phillips' view. "Republics," he said, "exist only on the tenure of being constantly agitated. The republic which sinks to sleep, trusting to constitutions and machinery, to politicians and statesmen, for the safety of its liberties, never will have any."[46]

But how can one account for the agitator or the negotiator—the Phillips or the Lincoln? All the factors enumerated to explain democratic and despotic man also seem to be required to explain why one person is an agitator and another a negotiator. Personality and character are unquestionably important: the inner needs of the agitator may feed on conflict, those of the negotiator on conciliation. Doubtless the agitator is often *driven* to seek conflict, the negotiator often *impelled* to seek concilia-tion.

But political culture also plays a part. In some countries, dominant cultural values strongly accent the desirability of obtaining widespread agreement, the virtues of consensus, hence the need to strive for concilia-tion and compromise, to avoid conflict.[47] As a person matures in such a culture, he is gradually socialized in its ways. He learns to behave as he is expected to behave. In some countries, then, he learns at an early age that it is better to negotiate than to agitate.

Yet even in a political culture marked by moderation and concilia-tion, a particular individual may deviate from the prevailing norms: his needs may drive him to defy the norms. More important, personal experi-ences and specific historical situations may alter his political practices, his orientations, even his life-style, and conceivably even the political culture.

Thus the rise of a new generation of black militants in the 1960s was more than a matter of particular personalities or a political culture; clearly the individual and collective experiences of black people and the historical situation of the 1960s played a decisive part. A substantial amount of evidence suggests that the white political activists of this pe-riod were different in some ways from other students, as persons; the radical activists, it appears, differed not only from the more conventional

---

[46]*Ibid.*, p. 138.

[47]Observers have frequently remarked on these qualities in Switzerland and the Scan-dinavian countries. See, for example, Harry Eckstein's description of Norwegian political norms in *Division and Cohesion in a Democracy: A Study of Norway* (Princeton, N. J.: Princeton University Press, 1966), p. 158 and passim. Putnam found British members of Parliament more likely to emphasize consensus, Italian members more likely to emphasize conflict (pp.. 101–105, 109–113).

student but also from the "alienated" student. Yet what crystallized their impulses toward activism was, surely, the historical situation in which they found themselves: widespread opulence and seemingly obsessive consumption confronting poverty, racial conflict, and a highly unpopular war in Viet-Nam sustained by compulsory military service.[48]

Varieties of Pragmatic Politicians. Even pragmatic politicians, of course, cannot be compressed into a single type. James D. Barber has suggested that American politicians in general and Presidents in particular display varying political styles along two dimensions:

> The first baseline in defining Presidential types is *activity-passivity*. How much energy does the man invest in his Presidency? Lyndon Johnson went at his day like a human cyclone, coming to rest long after the sun went down. Calvin Coolidge often slept eleven hours a night and still needed a nap in the middle of the day. . . . The second baseline is *positive-negative effect* toward one's activity, that is, how he feels about what he does. Relatively speaking, does he seem to experience his political life as happy or sad, enjoyable or discouraging, positive or negative in its main effect.[49]

These two dimensions produce "four basic character patterns long familiar in psychological research." These are the active-positive, the active-negative, the passive-positive, and the passive-negative.

> The first four Presidents, conveniently, ran through the gamut of character types. . . . Washington's dignity, judiciousness, his allover air of reserve and dedication to duty fit the passive-negative or withdrawing type best. . . . John Adams followed, a dour New England Puritan much given to work and worry, an impatient and irascible man—an active-negative President, a compulsive type. . . . Then came Jefferson . . . Jefferson was clearly active-positive. . . . Madison comes closest to the passive-positive, or compliant type. . . .[50]

How can we explain these different political styles? Barber conjectures that a political style typically emerges relatively early in life, in late adolescence or early manhood, when in some particular situations one's motives, resources, and opportunities combine to produce what appears

[48]Kenneth Keniston, *Young Radicals* (New York: Harcourt Brace Jovanovich, 1968), Appendix B, "The Sources of Student Dissent," pp. 297–325, at p. 309.

[49]James David Barber, *The Presidental Character: Predicting Performance in the White House* (Englewood Cliffs, N. J.: Prentice-Hall, 1972) pp. 11–14, and *passim*.

[50]James David Barber, *ibid.* In *The Lawmakers* (New Haven: Yale University Press, 1965) Barber used the typology to examine Connecticut legislators. For critique, see Alexander George, "Assessing Presidential Character," *World Politics* 26 (January 1974), pp. 234–282 and Erwin C. Hargrove, "Presidential Personality and Revisionist Views of the Presidency," *The American Journal of Political Science* 17 (November 1973), pp. 891–835.

to be a successful strategy, which then serves one for the rest of his life. Yet since motives, resources, and opportunities each vary over a wide range, "there is no one 'political man,' no universal pattern of leadership performance."[51]

Once again, the argument points to the conclusion that men who gain power need to be similar to one another only in certain formal respects. In fact, the concrete characteristics of leaders seem to vary a good deal in different cultures, political systems, times, and situations. Leaders have different social origins, resources, skills, and personalities.[52] Among those who have sought and gained power, the range runs from Napoleon Bonaparte, the Corsican upstart, to Winston Churchill, descendant of seven Dukes of Marlborough; from Caesar, the military genius, to Woodrow Wilson, historian, political scientist, and college president; from the detached and reflective Hadrian to Savonarola, the fanatic; from the regal Elizabeth I to Madam de Pompadour, the witty mistress of Louis XV; from the Serene stoicism of the philosopher Marcus Aurelius to the neurosis of Hitler and the paranoia of Stalin; from Caligua to Lincoln.

[51]James D. Barber, "Classifying and Predicting Presidential Styles: Two 'Weak' Presidents'" *The Journal of Social Issues* 24 (July 1968): 51–80.
[52]This conclusion recently has received further support from the emerging field of "psychohistory," in which an effort is made, usually by psychoanalysts or psychiatrists, to reconstruct the psychological dynamics of an historical figure or, in some cases, an historical movement. Two seminal sources are Alexander L. George and Juliette L. George, *Woodrow Wilson and Colonel House: A Personality Study* (New York: John Day, 1956), paperback edition with new preface, (New York: Dover Press, 1964), and Erik H. Erickson, *Young Man Luther* (New York: W. W. Norton & Co., 1958). For an account and some examples of psychohistory, see *Explorations in Psychohistory; the Wellfleet Papers*, ed. Robert Jay Lifton, with Eric Olson, and with essays by Erik Erikson and Kenneth Keniston (New York: Simon and Schuster, 1974).

CHAPTER   NINE

POLITICAL EVALUATION

One could passively contemplate politics, perhaps, without making decisions—but it would be extraordinarily difficult. Even deciding which of two or more alternative hypotheses is true requires a choice. In any case, one cannot participate actively in political life without making decisions. Indeed, is this not what we mean by political action? Political action, like other human actions, consists in making decisions—in somehow choosing among alternatives and then trying to make one's choices effective. Thus, in taking action, one is compelled to decide which alternative is best, or at least satisfactory. To make decisions intelligently, to choose wisely among alternatives, what kinds of knowledge does one need?

THE MAIN ELEMENTS IN POLITICAL EVALUATION

One's decisions are influenced by the way one appraises the world and one's place in it. Whenever a person makes a decision about buying a car, taking a job, going on a vacation, voting in an election, or confirming the relative desirability of democracy over dictatorship, one is making appraisals. In an abstract sense, the types of appraisals one makes are the same whether one decides among alternative political systems at the highly general level of political philosophy or tries to make a political decision in a specific situation. The substance and content of appraisals, of course, vary enormously. One is not likely to use the same information to make decisions about automobiles and presidential candidates. The quality of appraisals and the methods for making them also vary enormously. The appraisals on which a decision is based may be conscious or unconscious, simple or complex, deliberate or hasty, based on considerable information or little, wise or stupid.

What, then, are some of the principal appraisals that influence decisions?

One's decisions will be influenced by:

(1) what one considers to be the alternative courses of action that are open or available, if any;
(2) what one believes are the likely consequences of pursuing each of the alternative course of action; and
(3) the value one assigns to the consequences of each alternative.

These three appraisals are the most important ones in situations where one assumes that the consequences of each alternative are virtually certain to occur. But one generally cannot be certain of all the consequences. In situations of uncertainty, decisions often are influenced by several additional appraisals:

(4) One's guesses, hunches, or estimates concerning the probability that the various consequences will actually occur. Many differences in policy can be traced to differences in estimates of the likelihood of different consequences. Two people may agree substantially on the alternatives, the *possible* consequences of each, and on their evaluation of the different sets of consequences, and yet disagree on policy because their estimates concerning the likelihood of the consequences are different. In the United States, disagreements over appropriations for the Department of Defense ordinarily occur not because one side values peace more than the other, but because one side believes the likelihood of avoiding war is increased with larger defense expenditures while the other side believes that peace is just as likely, or even more likely, with lower expenditures.
(5) One's orientations *toward risk, uncertainty, and gambling.* A cautious person who only bets on a sure thing is unlikely to advocate the same policies as a more adventurous person who likes to take risks. (Of course a person who is adventurous in one situation may be cautious in another.) Despite the obvious importance of different orientations toward uncertainty, not much is known about them. Moreover, philosophers who have written about problems of ethics and values have not paid much attention to differences in orientations toward risk and uncertainty. Yet many differences over policies and decisions must depend on different orientations toward uncertainty.

Suppose you are confronted by two alternatives. One seems to offer almost an equal chance of brilliant success and dismal failure; if you choose the other, the chances of failure seem to be very small, but the gains, although relatively certain, are also very small. Is there a "rational" or "best" choice in cases like this? Is it more rational to invest in stocks and hope for large gains or to invest in bonds and count more confidently on small gains? Should one back a third-party candidate at the risk of bringing about the election of the worse of the two major-party candidates? Should one employ political tactics that offer the hope of influencing public opinion but run the risk of producing repression and counter-violence? Should one recommend international strategies that might increase the number of survivors in a nuclear war—but might also produce further escalation in the arms race and perhaps increase the chances of nuclear war?

For several generations, mathematicians, logicians, and others have sought to develop criteria of "rational" or "best" decisions for uncertain situations, using mathematical models derived from the theory of games and statistical decisions. Unfortunately, however, the more elegant and convincing the mathematical formulations, the more they apply to extremely simple human situations, and, therefore, the less they seem relevant to the complex problems of life. Conversely, when mathematicians attempt to grapple realistically with highly complex decisions, they find it necessary to introduce more and more assumptions resting on common sense, intuition, or their own personal values. For most crucial decisions, mathematical models have proved so far to be of little value.

Nonetheless, these recent developments in mathematics have emphasized much more sharply than philosophers had before that it is usually not enough to know which outcome is "the best" in order to make a decision. Ordinarily one cannot simply apply one's standards of values to the different possible results of a decision, determine which one is "the best," and then choose it. For if there is *uncertainty* about the outcomes, to choose "the best" might be to adopt a strategy that most people on careful reflection would surely reject. For example, let us suppose that one *possible* outcome of foreign policy A is an international system that will ensure permanent peace; but the most *likely* outcome of this policy is thermonuclear war. On the other hand, the most likely outcome of foreign policy B is another decade of stalemate without war or guaranteed peace. The chance that B will produce an international system of peace and order is virtually zero, yet the chance that it will lead to war is rather low. On reflection most people would, I suspect, prefer B to A, even though one possible result of A might be, in their view, far and away the "best" of all solutions.

NORMATIVE AND EMPIRICAL ANALYSIS

Of the five appraisals just discussed, two—the likely consequences of each alternative and the relative probability that these consequences actually will ensue—require empirical analysis. Both involve an element of prediction: if x happens, then (probably) y will happen. Predictions are the domain of the empirical sciences rather than of philosophy, religion, or ethics.

By contrast, to judge the value of each alternative we confront and to appraise alternatives in situations of risk and uncertainty evidently require beliefs or assumptions as to value, goodness, or moral worth. Any systematic examination of those assumptions requires—and *is*—normative analysis.

In practice political decisions usually entail a mixture of empirical and moral judgments. Indeed, one of the five appraisals listed above seems to be a mixture. In one sense, to judge what alternative courses of action are open or available is a judgment of fact that requires empirical evidence. For example: Am I legally entitled to vote in the coming election? Is it too late now to nominate a new candidate? Yet because the possible actions "open" to me (in some sense) seem almost infinite, to judge which actions are also *relevant* to my purposes, I need to take into account what I believe to be good or valuable.

Can we, however, distinguish between good and bad or better and worse decisions? And to the extent that these rest on political analysis, what can we say about the *quality* of empirical and normative analysis?

The Quality of Empirical Analysis
For purposes of action, an empirical analysis falls short of what we want from it if it leads to wrong predictions or, putting it another way, if it leads to expectations about the future that are falsified by events. How to improve the quality of predictions (and of empirical analysis more generally) and what limits to the discovery of regularities may exist because of the special characteristics of human beings and societies, are topics too vast in scope for treatment here. It seems fair to suggest, however, that success in producing reliable predictive knowledge might serve as one reasonable test for the quality of the empirical analysis used in making a decision.

Judged by this test, the quality of empirical knowledge needed for political action usually is far below the requirements of rational, or even highly informed, action. It is quite clear that reliable predictive knowledge about human and social systems has been very much harder to gain than reliable empirical knowledge about physical or strictly biological systems. Hence, much of the predictive knowledge used in making political decisions must be, in the absence of anything better, at a relatively low level of reliability. Much political knowledge is prescientific or nonscientific in character; often one must draw on prevailing common sense notions (with full awareness that the common sense of one generation is frequently seen as childish nonsense by a later generation). Often, too, one must rely on inference from a woefully limited and unanalyzed body of experiences. A person who refuses to make political decisions unless they are based on empirical knowledge at a high level of scientific validity will be paralyzed. Yet in politics "refusing to decide" is simply deciding to allow others to decide for you. Hence, anyone who makes political decisions usually must act on very incomplete factual information. Uncertainty as to the facts and difficulty in arriving at correct factual judgments are among the most familiar elements in the life of the political decision-maker, whether one is an ordinary citizen or the President of the United States.

The Quality of Normative Analysis

Is there a criterion for evaluating the quality of normative analysis that can serve in the same way that predictability can serve for empirical analysis? If, as stated in Chapter Two, any extended normative analysis usually presupposes some empirical belief, then normative analysis is bound to entail some of the uncertainties that cloud our empirical knowledge, or lack of it. The core of the normative orientation, however, is a concern for what ought to be. I want to know which alternative, among those I think confront me in a particular situation, is best or at least better. Therefore, I need a standard (or standards) of value, a criterion for judging which alternative is better, best, good, or right.[1]

If I have the end in mind and need only to make a judgment among alternative means, I may be satisfied with judgments about instrumental value. For example, I might recommend: "If we want to increase the turnout in Presidential elections, the best way would be to reduce the difficulties in registering to vote." The quality of judgments about instrumental value evidently depends in some measure on the quality of the empirical analysis they presuppose. Yet sooner or later, judgments of value seem to require one to believe that some things are intrinsically valuable or good in themselves.[2] Suppose, for example, someone who

[1]For a recent statement, see Brian Barry and Douglas Rae, "Political Evaluation," in *The Handbook of Political Science* (Reading, Mass.: Addison-Wesley Publishing Co., 1975).

[2]This distinction is as old as philosophical discourse. It is clearly set out in the opening pages of Aristotle's *Ethics*. See Aristotle, *Ethics* (London: Penquin Books, 1953), p. 34.

had asserted: "Democracy is the best form of government" were asked, "Why—on what grounds—do you believe that?" He might reply, "Democracy is the only form of government that secures political equality. And political equality is better than political inequality." Suppose a persistent questioner demands to know the grounds for this belief? One might introduce still another criterion and contend that political equality was necessary to fulfill that criterion—for example, to achieve happiness, or consent for laws, or general equality—or one might say that political equality is intrinsically valuable, good in itself.

Most people might be satisfied with such an answer, but philosophers characteristically are not. A philosophically inclined and very persistent questioner, therefore, might ask: "But how do we *know* that political equality (or happiness, consent, general equality, or anything else) is intrinsically valuable? In short, what are your grounds for believing so?" This is a formidable question, one of the oldest and most difficult in political philosophy, and there is no consensus on the answers. Perhaps none of the philosophical underpinnings of political analysis has been subject in recent decades to so much controversy.

The main viewpoints are:[3]

(1) *Naturalism,* which holds that certain moral principles or value statements are true because they are descriptions of universal properties of man. Thus one might contend that since everyone seeks happiness, it is absurd to deny that happiness is intrinsically good. Or one might argue that since everyone (or practically everyone) wishes to survive, survival must be regarded as intrinsically good and destruction of human life as intrinsically evil. Starting from a belief in the intrinsic worth of happiness, or human survival, one might then elaborate a moral code, a set of "natural laws," consisting of actions that are *extrinsically* or *instrumentally* good because they lead to happiness (or survival).

Thus naturalism closes most of the gap between value judgments and factual judgments. For whatever men universally seek is held to be good. And what it is that men universally seek requires, in essence, only a factual judgment. Seen in this context, empirical knowledge can be

---

[3]In the ensuing discussion, I have followed categories, to which I have added a fourth, suggested by Felix E. Oppenheim in *Moral Principles in Policial Philosophy* (New York: Random House, 1968). For a roughly parallel discussion, see William K. Frankena, *Ethics,* 2nd ed. (Englewood Cliffs, N.J.: Prentice-Hall, 1973), Chapter Six, "Meaning and Justification," pp. 95–116. Writers on ethics classify ethical systems in various ways; there is no standard or generally accepted typology. Two useful introductions are Bernard Williams, *Morality: An Introduction to Ethics* (New York: Harper Torchbooks, 1972) and Fred M. Frohock, *Normative Political Theory,* in this series. An excellent history with a strong focus on ethics in political philosophy is Alasdair MacIntyre, *A Short History of Ethics* (New York: Macmillan Co., 1966).

readily converted into—is, in fact, the principal component of—moral action.

Because naturalism can make ready use of factual knowledge, Frederick M. Watkins, an exponent of this approach in political analysis, argued that:

> Modern science, by vastly expanding our knowledge of [human] nature and of [human] needs, provides the basis for a number of verifiable propositions which enable us, more adequately than ever before, to define the potentialities and limits of human action. These propositions, I believe, are entirely adequate to provide a basis for the kind of normative enquiry that former ages followed in their discussions of natural law.[4]

(2) *Intuitionism* holds that although the quality of goodness cannot be perceived by the ordinary senses, man is endowed with a special capacity for apprehending intrinsic goodness. As some advocates of intuitionism would say, man's sixth sense is his insight into good and evil. Thus just as man's insight gives him confidence in the elementary rules of logic, it can also yield conclusions as compelling as any rule of logic. To some intuitionists, like St. Augustine, insight reveals knowledge of God and His moral truths. But an intuitionist need not be religious; to some intuitionists, like Plato and Rousseau, insight discloses knowledge of an excellence that is not necessarily God's law but an inherent part of the structure of the universe. Some intuitionists argue, as did St. Thomas Aquinas, that the process is not so much one of immediate intuition, or of sudden revelation, but a product of reason, like mathematics. In this view, some moral principles are self-evident. They are obviously true because they cannot be denied logically: denial involves self-contradiction. Once one possesses these self-evident first principles, one can then use deductive reasoning—sheer logic—to derive specific principles of right or wrong. In a similar spirit Immanuel Kant arrived at his famous "categorical imperative," which he believed to be a rationally demonstrable principle that one could not deny without inconsistency: "There is, therefore, only one categorical imperative. It is: Act only according to that maxim by which you can at the same time will that it should become a universal law."[5]

(3) *Noncognitivism or subjectivism* are names some philosophers give to the view that, unlike factual assertions, assertions about intrinsic value

---

[4]Frederick M. Watkins, "Natural Law and the Problem of Value-Judgments," in *Political Research and Political Theory* ed. Oliver Garceau (Cambridge, Mass.: Harvard University Press, 1968), pp. 58–74, at pp. 69–72. See also Abraham Edel, "Ethical Judgment," in *The Use of Science in Ethics* (New York: The Free Press, 1964).

[5]From *Metaphysics of Morals* (1785), quoted in Oppenheim, *Moral Principles*, p. 90.

cannot be shown to be true of false.[6] Efforts made by advocates of naturalism, intuitionism, and natural law to prove that moral principles are objectively valid can be demonstrated, noncognitivists argue, to be inadequate. Statements about intrinsic values, they contend, are assertions of belief. They may reveal one's orientations or intentions toward the world and toward one's fellow creatures; but unlike factual judgments, they lack the "cognitive status" of objective propositions; hence the name noncognitivism.

Although critics of noncognitivism sometimes portray it as nihilism or worse, noncognitive views, like naturalism and intuitionism, are held by people of quite diverse political philosophies. Probably the outstanding example of a noncognitivist approach to political theory is that of Thomas Hobbes, who was, politically speaking, a monarchist. Though Machiavelli never elaborated his views on this matter, he also appears to have been a noncognitivist—and a deeply convinced republican. John Stuart Mill's commitment to happiness as the supreme good seems to place him in the camp of naturalism; but the tenor of his argument brings him very close at times to a subjectivist position. Modern existentialists, whether religious, nonreligious, or antireligious, are frequently subjectivists. In a famous lecture given in 1946, the French writer and Philosopher Jean-Paul Sartre contended, "existentialism is a humanism." He stated:

> Man is nothing else but that which he makes of himself. That is the first principle of existentialism. . . . Thus, the first effect of existentialism is that it puts every man in possession of himself as he is, and places the entire responsibility for his existence squarely upon his own shoulders. And, when we say that man is responsible for himself, we do not mean that he is responsible only for his own individuality, but that he is responsible for all men. . . . Who, then, can prove that I am the proper person to impose, by my own choice, my conception of man upon mankind? I shall never find any proof whatever; there will be no sign to convince me of it. . . . If I regard a certain course of action as good, it is only I who choose to say that it is good and not bad. . . .[7]

(4) *Semantic analysis.* A fourth approach, one not inherently inconsistent with any one of the three perspectives just described, has recently

---

[6]Frankena, who points out that this "third general type of theory . . . has no very satisfactory label," notes that it is called both noncognitivist and nondescriptivist. *Ethics*, p. 105. Williams refers instead to "subjectivism." *Morality*, pp. 13 ff.

[7]Jean-Paul Sartre, "Existentialism Is a Humanism," reprinted in W. Kaufmann, ed., *Existentialism from Dostoevsky to Sartre* (Cleveland: Meridian Books, 1956), pp. 287–311, at pp. 290–293. Sartre has since repudiated some of the statements in this lecture.

gained ground in political evaluation. This is semantic analysis, the analysis of meaning. Semantic analysis in moral and political evaluation is strongly influenced by the later work of the philosopher Ludwig Wittgenstein (1889–1951).[8] In general, semantic analysis seeks the meaning of moral terms as these are actually used in ordinary, nonphilosophical language. As a result of their reflections on how we express our meaning when we wish to indicate moral and evaluative judgments, as distinguished from judgments about matters in the domain of empirical science, some writers conclude that language is in effect divided into different "regions." The languages of different "regions" deal with different matters. The language of one region is often inappropriate and confusing when it is applied to matters requiring a rather different sort of language. One such region, it is suggested, is moral discourse. To rely exclusively on the language of the empirical sciences to explore the domain of moral discourse (as, it is argued, some noncognitivists propose to do) is fundamentally as absurd as using the language of physics or chemistry in order to discuss the esthetic qualities of a painting.

In the argument between Thrasymachus and Socrates discussed in Chapter 8,[9] for example, a possible interpretation by means of semantic analysis is that:

> Though there is a dispute here, it is not between what is and what ought to be, nor between facts and values . . . One might say that Thrasymachus is talking about the facts of what people consider just, and Socrates about what they ought to consider just in the light of the meaning of 'justice.' But the meaning of 'justice' depends on the facts of its grammar, so this is a dispute about facts, over the implications of two different kinds of facts. It depends on there being an inconsistency in the grammar of 'justice,' between what people consider just and what the word 'justice' means.[10]

One aim of this approach—with some practitioners the exclusive aim—is to enrich and clarify moral discourse and political evaluation by heightening our understanding of the language we use when we discuss moral questions, as practically everyone does. Although a great deal of "ordinary language philosophy" is tedious and often seems trivial, at its best semantic analysis seeks to restore the dignity and significance to

---

[8]Wittgenstein's later work is somewhat at odds with his earlier work, which strongly influenced logical positivism and the spread of subjectivism in ethics.

[9]Supra, p. 111.

[10]Hanna Fenichel Pitkin, *Wittgenstein and Justice* (Berkeley: University of California Press, 1972), p. 187.

political evaluation, and to moral discourse generally, that were eroded as naturalism and intuitionism lost out to subjectivism.[11]

In some versions, semantic analysis of moral discourse can be interpreted as a new form of naturalism.[12] Yet it would be going too far to say that semantic analysis has overcome the clash among the approaches of naturalism, intuitionism, and noncognitivism. Indeed, the conflict seems too fundamental to be resolved by general agreement. An individual may resolve it for himself by opting for one view or the other, but it seems highly unlikely that everyone will ever hold the same view. Hence normative political analysis seems destined to remain forever a battlefield in which champions of sharply clashing views vainly seek to gain lasting supremacy over their opponents.

Decline and Revival of Normative Theory

The persistence of conflicting perspectives in the domain of normative political theory is not necessarily a symptom of ill-health. Some would see it as a sign of vigor. A serious problem does arise, however, if normative analysis is simply ignored. For several generations, this appeared to be the fate of normative political theory.

The decline of normative analysis was partly a product of changes in the way moral argument came to be understood in the modern world among philosophers and, in a less professional or systematic fashion, among intellectuals and other people as well.

Until the nineteenth century, in the Western world various forms of naturalism and intuitionism were widely subscribed to by political philosophers, and probably by many others. Whether morality was held to be derived from nature, intuition, or revelation, it was believed to contain some of the objectivity and certainty of empirical knowledge. Since the latter part of the nineteenth century and increasingly in the twentieth—the views of Friedrich Wilhelm Nietzsche (1844–1900) often are seen as a turning point—subjectivist or noncognitivist views have tended to prevail among philosophers and most likely among large sections of the political stratum in all modern societies. Under the impact of these beliefs, normative political analysis decayed.

[11]Although less directly influenced by Wittgenstein, Brian Barry, *Political Argument* (New York: The Humanities Press, 1967) also stresses and exemplifies the possibilities of clarifying political judgments through (in part) the meticulous analysis of meaning.

[12]Frohock refers to it as "the new naturalism," pp. 23–43, *op. cit.* Cf. also David Pears, *Ludwig Wittgenstein* (New York: The Viking Press, 1969, 1970): ". . . (I)n general his philosophy is a kind of psychological naturalism. Wittgenstein's later philosophy is another species in the same genus: it is not psychological naturalism, but linguistic naturalism," p. 184.

By contrast, for about a generation after World War II, empirical political analysis flourished. Echoing a position sometimes advanced by the philosophical school of logical positivism,[13] political scientists engaged in empirical analysis sometimes concluded that since statements about values could neither be "objectively" verified nor falsified (and hence were radically more subjective than empirical propositions) moral argument must be inherently meaningless. Normative political analysis was therefore irrelevant at best and downright obfuscating at worst.

Meanwhile, the growth of new normative political theories languished. Philosophers were involved mainly in intricate arguments over the grounds, if any, for moral argument—in *metaethics* rather than in ethics itself. In political science departments, normative political analysis consisted (and still does) mostly of interpreting and re-interpreting the great political theories of the past. Interpreters of these works often insisted on their relevance and importance for political analysis. For all their insistence that moral argument was meaningful, however, they rarely undertook the formidable task of developing a convincing demonstration of the validity of a concrete moral argument. They tended to assert the *possibility* of moral argument but did not demonstrate it successfully by example, nor did they seek to construct a normative theory of their own based on the model of the past giants they admired.

Although there were exceptions they were few and not widely influential. There are signs, however, that normative political theory (which seems to thrive best when accepted beliefs are crumbling) may have begun a revival in the 1970s. One indication was the publication in 1971 of John Rawls' *A Theory of Justice* (Cambridge, Mass.: Harvard University Press) which not only triggered off an unprecedented amount of interest and critical comment but, more significantly, shifted the focus of the discussion away from the dominant metaethical question—whether reasoning about moral principles is meaningful and fruitful—to a controversy over the validity of the specific principles of justice he had advanced. In its substance and vigor, the discussion itself gave persuasive testimony to a widely held if largely implicit belief that reasoning about moral principles is indeed meaningful and important.[14]

---

[13]A highly readable, straightforward, widely read, and enormously influential work was A. J. Ayer's *Language, Truth and Logic* (London: Gollancz, 1936, and New York: Dover Press, 1946). Although Ayer has modified some of his views, he has remained a subjectivist (or noncognitivist) in ethics. See *The Central Question of Philosophy* (New York: Holt, Rinehart and Winston, 1973), pp. 226–227.

[14]The appearance in 1975 of Robert Nozick's *Anarchy, State and Utopia* (New York: Basic Books) may be another straw in the wind.

The Function of Clarification

The subjectivist critique of the foundations of moral belief has not, however, been answered conclusively, nor is it likely to be. As I have suggested already, controversies among advocates of naturalism, intuitionism, and subjectivism seem likely to continue indefinitely.

Yet it does not follow that because the most basic foundations of our knowledge about ethics seem destined to remain controversial—and for many of us, uncertain—moral argument is inherently meaningless or that normative political analysis must be irrelevant or obfuscating. Because normative analysis can neither eliminate uncertainty in moral decisions nor promise conclusive answers to all ethical dilemmas hardly seems a valid reason for rejecting it. Perhaps the only certainty about political life, after all, is the prevalence of uncertainty.

In the midst of uncertainty, one contribution of normative analysis can be—and at its best is—that of clarification: to help us understand the grounds on which we stand, the principles to which we commit ourselves, the relations among our principles—their consistency or conflict—the nature of the alternatives we confront, and, finally, which alternative is the best and our reasons for believing so.

CHAPTER TEN

CHOOSING POLICIES: STRATEGIES OF INQUIRY AND DECISION

When deciding on a policy one is attempting to narrow the distance between where one is and where one wants to be. A policy, then, is a bridge between what one thinks will be if one does not act and what one believes ought to be. It is a path to the best alternative a person can obtain at a cost one is willing to pay, and it requires both empirical and normative analysis.

The act of adopting a policy, particularly an important policy, is nearly always surrounded by a cloud of uncertainty. We are uncertain as to matters of fact: If we elect X, what will he actually do in office? Are the policies I want more likely to be achieved through a third party than through one of the major parties? Is the society I desire more likely to be fostered by increasing participation in politics? If so, what can I do to expand participation? Would the use of violence for specific ends I favor significantly increase the chances of a repressive reaction?

We are often uncertain, too, as to matters of value: If decentralization, which I favor, leads to less racial integration, which I also favor, where do I stand? Is coercive violence, which I regard as intrinsically evil, ever justified—as in the American Revolution or the Civil War? If not, am I simply permitting coercive violence by others? If so, in what circumstances? When, if ever, is intolerance of opinion or advocacy justified in a democracy?

Uncertainty over the answers to questions like these, and there are thousands of such questions, seems to be inherent in political life. What strategies of inquiry help to improve the quality of one's political decisions amid the inevitable uncertainties?

Strategies of Pure Science. There is a long-enduring and apparently irrepressible hope among students of politics that a choice among different political alternatives can be based on a pure science of politics. In earlier times, this pure science was to have included not only the factual or empirical elements, as in physics or chemistry, but also the normative or evaluational elements. In this century, however, as the term "science" increasingly has come to mean *empirical* science, the aspiration toward a pure science of politics has come to mean an empirical science of politics. According to this view, an empirical science of politics would be concerned exclusively with the validity of the factual or empirical elements. To be sure, its knowledge would be applied in action; but the validity of the ends, goals, or values sought in action would, as such, lie outside the domain of the pure science.

Some advocates of a pure science of politics believe, like the noncognitivists, that although there are scientific procedures for establishing the objective validity of empirical propositions, no procedures exist for determining the objective truth or falsity of a statement asserting that something is good or valuable. But the idea of a pure science of politics is not necessarily opposed by those who adhere to positions of naturalism or intuitionism. After all, one who believes in the value of health would probably want an empirical science of medicine that a doctor might use to cure a sick patient. So, too, one who believes that equality, for example, is objectively better than inequality might advocate an empirical science of politics that would, among other things, provide reliable scientific knowledge about the conditions that facilitate or hinder the fullest measure of human equality. In fact, as Frederick Watkins pointed out in the quotation cited in Chapter Nine, the attempt to discover the modern equivalent of "natural law" requires the help of modern science in order "to define the potentialities and limits of human action."

Is a pure science of politics possible or desirable? Like all the other questions touched on in this chapter, this too is vigorously contested. Lack of space prevents us from exploring the major issues here.[1] Nonetheless, if only to illustrate the complexities of the argument, it may be useful to take a brief look at several of the issues.

Can Political Phenomena Be Measured? As everyone knows, discoveries in the natural sciences have been greatly aided by possibilities of measurement. Nature, it has been said, loves quantity. One key subject of dispute is the extent to which valid and reliable measures, comparable to

---

[1]Cf. J. Donald Moon, "The Logic of Political Inquiry: A Synthesis of Opposed Perspectives," in *The Handbook of Political Science*, ed. Fred I. Greenstein and Nelson W. Polsby (Reading, Mass.: Addison-Wesley Publishing Co., 1975). Further references are found below on p. 150.

Figure 10

those used in the natural sciences, can be developed for political phenomena.

In politics as elsewhere it is an enormous and obvious advantage to be able to measure differences. Suppose one is wrestling with the question of what political system is best. One might then wish to know what difference it makes whether a system is a polyarchy or one of the many alternatives to polyarchy.

Consider the familiar way of analyzing experience symbolized in Figure 10. The paradigm is commonplace not only in the natural sciences, in medicine, and in the social and behavioral sciences but also in everyday life. In Chapter Five, we applied it to political systems; we can also apply it to political evaluation. Suppose, for example, that differences in "coercion," "conflict," or "personal freedom" are thought to be important. We may then want to know whether differences in characteristics of political systems (II) have consequences for "coercion," "conflict," or "personal freedom" (I). If they do, then we also may want to know what conditions (III) are likely to bring about or prevent the development of a "freedom-enhancing" system, or a "minimal-coercion" system, or a peaceful-settlement" system. This kind of thinking is *causal analysis*, the attempt to understand causes.[2] In politics, as in medicine, one wants to understand causes in order to obtain desired results, such as enhanced freedom, greater equality, more security, less coercion, greater social peace, or other goals.

But how can we find out what changes in conditions (III) produce variations in systems (II), which in turn lead to differences in consequences (I)? For self-evident reasons, politics largely excludes the possibility of experimentation in a strict sense. Fortunately, however, good logical approximations to experimentation can be made by the application of rather powerful quantitative methods—provided the data are in quantitative form. One recent innovation in political analysis—both a

[2]A succinct and lucid introduction to causal analysis is Arthur L. Stenchcombe's discussion in *Constructing Social Theories* (New York: Harcourt Brace Jovanovich, 1968), pp. 28–38.

cause and an effect of the flood of data—is a vigorous attempt to develop ways of measuring political phenomena to provide quantitative and not merely qualitative data bearing on relevant differences.

Some of the older skepticism about quantitative data was a product of rather unsophisticated ideas about measurement. Most people think of "measurement" only in terms of what specialists on measurement call *interval*-measures, like those used for height, weight, population, area, and so on. Although interval-measures are used for some phenomena relevant to differences in political systems—rates of voter turnout in elections, for example—most political phenomena are subject at best only to *ordinal* measurement, that is, a ranking according to "more," "equal," or "less." Fortunately, ranking or ordinal measurement also allows powerful quantitative methods to be used on data.

One advantage of quantitative data, then, is that they greatly facilitate causal analysis. A second advantage is that quantitative data can be much more efficiently analyzed than qualitative data, particularly with the aid of high-speed computers. Quantitive methods thus offer a possible way of coping with the flood of data about political systems that now threatens to inundate us. Although the prospect seems slight that quantitative methods will ever entirely displace the more familiar methods of qualitative analysis, it is hardly open to doubt that in the future political analysis will have to make far more use of quantitative data and methods than it has in the past.[3]

When Does a Difference "Make a Difference"? When is a difference trivial and when does it matter? One can rapidly traverse a very small circle right back to the starting point: a difference matters if one thinks that directly or indirectly it has large enough consequences for one's values. Large enough for what? Large enough to matter.

In political controversy it is not always possible to break out of this circle. What is important to one observer sometimes seems utterly trivial to another. To many an American the differences between "democracy" as practiced in the United States and "socialist democracy" as practiced in the Soviet Union are highly important. To an anarchist, the differences might seem to be trivial variations in two oppressively authoritarian systems.

If disagreement as to whether a difference is trivial or important cannot *always* be settled, dispute of this kind *sometimes* can be profitably bypassed. For in practice many people do share similar views about the relative importance of certain differences. Moreover, a solution satisfactory to all can sometimes be obtained by an analysis that takes into

[3]The subject of measurement and quantitative political analysis is vast, and the discussion here necessarily skims the surface. The topic is treated much more extensively in the volume in this series by Edward R. Tufte, *Data Analysis for Politics and Policy.*

account *all* the differences thought to be relevant. An explanation of why different modern societies develop such varying political systems as inclusive polyarchies, competitive oligarchies, conservative authoritarian regimes, and modernizing dictatorships would be important to advocates of each type of system. These considerations suggest an obvious but not trivial conclusion: with respect to any characteristic on which political systems differ, the greater the amount of variation or difference one's analysis can explain, the more useful or "powerful" the analysis is.

Yet the question remains whether "important" differences in political phenomena can be measured adequately. Clearly the utility of a science of politics depends heavily on the answer to this question. In arriving at an answer, the reader may wish to reflect on evidence contained in several of the earlier chapters in this book, particularly Chapters Six and Seven. Only a few years ago, attempts to measure the amount of "conflict" or "pluralism" in a country would have been regarded by most political scientists as absurd. They are still so regarded by many; but an increasing minority argue that even inadequate quantitative data are useful supplements to qualitative judgments that often rest upon highly impressionistic evidence.

Nonetheless, it would be premature to conclude that you will soon be able to make political choices on factual appraisals as solid as those in the natural sciences or engineering. There seems to be no satisfactory way to predict the rate at which factual knowledge required for political choices will increase. It is reasonable to conjecture that the flood of data now inundating us will in time be matched by an increase in verified hypotheses and theories. But the history of the natural sciences suggests that more data do not lead automatically to the discovery of nature's regularities.

Even under highly optimistic assumptions about the rate of increase in our factual knowledge, it seems quite clear that at present and in the near future a great many political choices are bound to be surrounded by a cloud of uncertainty. For in comparison with the natural sciences, medicine, or engineering, where judgments about the value, moral quality, or goodness of different alternatives are ordinarily absent or relatively simple, in politics moral judgments are pervasive, powerful, and complex. The relative importance of a "fact," as we have seen, depends on one's standard of value.

Holistic Strategies. Since political choices are usually clouded by uncertainties, some students of decision making have tried to develop strategies realistically adapted to situations of limited knowledge. Their approach is best seen as a reaction to strategies of perfect rationality, sometimes called *synoptic* or *holistic* approaches, that emphasize the desirability of a complete search for a rational answer before a choice is made. What is sometimes thought to be the ideal strategy of perfect rationality has been described as follows:

1. Faced with a given problem,
2. a rational man first clarifies his goals, values, or objectives, and then ranks or otherwise organizes them in his mind;
3. he then lists all important possible ways of—policies for—achieving his goals
4. and investigates all the important consequences that would follow from each of the alternative policies,
5. at which point he is in a position to compare consequences of each policy with goals
6. And so choose the policy with consequences most closely matching his goals.[4]

This kind of strategy has great appeal—in the abstract. Yet in practice it is hardly more than a definition of perfect rationality; and perfect rationality has been unattainable, in politics as elsewhere. In practice, one is probably never in a position to acquire all the knowledge one needs for a completely rational decision on significant political questions.

Even if in practice a synoptic or holistic strategy is impossible to carry out completely, is it not, nevertheless, the ideal strategy? Even if we know we must fall short of perfect rationality, does not the synoptic strategy provide us with the model toward which we should aspire? Although the affirmative answer is tempting and plausible, in recent years critics have argued that the synoptic model is highly misleading. While it might provide a definition of perfect rationality, as a model for decision making it is generally useless or even downright harmful.

Critics of the synoptic model[5] contend that in practice decision-makers rarely if ever go through the steps outlined above. Because of limitations in our knowledge decisions are made and *must* be made in the midst of uncertainties. If we postponed decisions until we approached perfect rationality we would never make a decision.

Strategies of Limited Rationality

In practice, one manages to cope with uncertainty in a number of useful ways. You search for satisfactory rather than perfect solutions to problems. You make a tentative decision and see what happens. You take

---

[4]Lindblom, *The Policy-Making Process,* in this series p. 13.

[5]A leading critic of synoptic approaches to decision making and an advocate of limited strategies is Charles E. Lindblom, whose views will be found *ibid.,* particularly at pp. 14–27, and in D. Braybrooke and C. E. Lindblom, *A Strategy of Decision* (New York: Free Press, 1963).

advantage of feedback, or information created by the initial decision itself.[6] As a result of feedback, you can change your goals, even highly important goals. You can usually assume, too, that the decision you will make is an endless series of steps, so that your errors can be corrected as you proceed. Thus frequently you can adopt an "incrementalist" strategy: starting with an existing state of affairs about which a good deal is known, you can make small or incremental changes in the desired direction and then see what the next steps should be. You can go on making incremental changes indefinitely. A series of incremental changes can, in time, add up to a profound transformation: If you increase anything at the rate of 5 percent a year, you will double it in fourteen years.

Strategies that aim at perfect rationality are plausible and appealing, but they seem virtually impossible to execute. Strategies that aim at limited rationality seem somehow less "rational": yet in most situations limited strategies are all that you or anyone else will have for making decisions.

Experimental Strategies

Troubled by the high degree of uncertainty surrounding policy making by governments, the comparatively low level of reliable knowledge on which decisions must be based, and palpable failures in policies produced both by holistic and by incremental strategies, some political analysts have begun to emphasize the possibility of reducing ignorance and uncertainty in policy making by deliberate experimentation, or small-scale tryouts prior to the adoption of policies.

Obviously not all crucial decisions can be preceded by a small-scale tryout. Foreign policies, for example, hardly lend themselves to prior experimentation. The idea also creates images of inhumane experiments with powerless victims such as prisoners who may be coerced into participating or ill-informed subjects whose "consent" is gained by manipulative persuasion.

Proponents of experimentalism in policy making point out, however, that in practice governments do make decisions on a variety of matters with wholly inadequate knowledge about the results to be expected. Not only are policies adopted that would be rejected if the results had been correctly foreseen; policies are also rejected that would have been adopted if the outcomes were better understood. Adopting or rejecting policy alternatives has favorable and harmful consequences for millions of people and costs in both private and public outlays billions of dollars. Thus policy decisions do in fact "experiment" with the welfare

[6]See Karl W. Deutsch, *The Nerves of Government* (New York: Free Press, 1963), Chapter Eleven, "Government as a Process of Steering: The Concepts of Feedback, Goal, and Purpose," pp. 182–199.

and happiness of people. But this experimentation is large scale, costly, and lacks all the criteria of a scientific experiment designed to produce reliable knowledge. Hence, often it would be feasible and much more reasonable, it is argued, to run small-scale, controlled, carefully studied tryouts in advance.[7]

Searching for Alternatives. None of these strategies can guarantee that it will lead to the discovery of the best available alternatives. As in the arts, in science, in mathematics, or in the exploration of space, discovery requires an imaginative search.

There is, then, an indispensable need in political analysis for the informed imagination; for speculation, guided by knowledge, that transcends the received truths; for the design and contemplation of Utopias; for a willingness to think hard about unthinkable alternatives to all the too easily thinkable solutions. There is, in short, a need for a creative search inspired by the hunch that somewhere between the unattainable best and the kind of mediocrity so often attained in political matters there lies a universe of better alternatives—and worse ones, too—all waiting to be explored.

[7]The Brookings Institution, Washington, D.C., has a Panel on Social Experimentation to "assess the usefulness of experiments as a way of increasing knowledge about the effects of domestic social policies and programs of the federal government." Studies include Edward M. Gramlich and Patricia P. Koshel, *Educational Performance Contracting: An Evaluation of an Experiment* (1975); Joseph A. Pechman and P. Michael Timpane, eds., *Work Incentives and Income Guarantees: The New Jersey Negative Income Tax Experiment* (1975); and Alice M. Rivlin and P. Michael Timpane, eds., *Planned Variation: Should We Give Up or Try Harder?* (1975).

TO EXPLORE
FURTHER

The reader who wishes to explore topics touched on in this book should consult the footnotes, for I have cited those references not so much to provide authority for what I have written as to indicate where the interested reader might go for further information.

An important source published in 1975, and hence not available for previous editions of this book, is *The Handbook of Political Science*, ed. Fred I. Greenstein and Nelson W. Polsby, 8 vols. (Reading, Mass.: Addison-Wesley Publishing Co.). Although I have cited only a few of the *Handbook* articles in the footnotes, there are articles in the eight volumes that touch on practically every chapter in this book.

For the reader who may wish to go beyond the *Handbook* and the works cited in the footnotes, a few additional references may be helpful.

A great number of books and articles are directly relevant to the matters covered in Chapter Three, "Political Influence," and Chapter Four, "Forms of Influence." Nagel's book, cited in footnote 6, contains a lengthy and up-to-date bibliography. A useful collection of articles will be found in Roderick Bell, David V. Edwards, and R. Harrison Wagner, *Political Power, A Reader in Theory and Research* (New York: Free Press, 1969), which also has a good bibliography. Other analyses, and bibliographies will be found in Andrew S. McFarland, *Power and Leadership in Pluralist Systems* (Stanford, Calif.: Stanford University Press, 1969); and William A. Gamson, *Power and Discontent* (Homewood, Ill.: Dorsey Press, 1968); and my article "Power" in the *International Encyclopedia of the Social Sciences*, ed. David L. Sills (New York: Macmillan Co. and Free Press, 1968).

A book critical of some of my own earlier formulations is Steven Lukes, *Power: A Radical View* (London: Macmillan & Co., 1974). The topic discussed in Chapter Four is explored from a perspective somewhat different from my own by David V. J. Bell in *Power, Influence, and Authority* (New York: Oxford University Press, 1975).

Important contributions to our understanding of the similarities differences, and development of political systems will be found in volume 3 of *The Handbook of Political Science*. See in particular Samuel P. Huntington and Jorge I. Dominguez, "Political Development," Juan J. Linz, "Totalitarian and Authoritarian Regimes," and Charles Tilly, "Revolutions and Collective Violence." A collection of essays on one-party systems is in Samuel P. Huntington and Clement H. Moore, *Authoritarian Politics in Modern Society* (New York: Basic Books, 1970). A highly influential book on the nature of political development is Huntington's *Political Order in Changing Societies* (New Haven: Yale University Press, 1968).

In addition to the work cited in the footnote in Chapter Eight, "Political Man," Verba and Nie have contributed an article "Political Participation" to volume 4 of the *Handbook*. The volume also contains Philip E. Converse, "Public Opinion and Voting Behavior." In volume 3, a particularly relevant article is David O. Sears, "Political Socialization."

Political Evaluation (Chapter Nine) is the subject of voluminous and controversial literature. One would be well advised to begin by consulting Frohock's volume in this series, the work by Barry and Rae cited in footnote 1, page 132, and the works cited in footnote 3, p. 133.

An older conflict that stirred political scientists for many years is reflected in Arnold Brecht's *Political Theory: The Foundations of Twentieth Century Political Thought* (Princeton, N.J.: Princeton University Press, 1959), which contains an extensive statement of the issues, the history of the conflict, the different views, and his own position, which he calls Scientific Value Relativism. The most thoroughgoing criticism of the position represented by Brecht is contained in Herbert J. Storing ed., *Essays on the Scientific Study of Politics* (New York: Henry Holt & Co., 1961), which contains four essays critically examining the voting studies and the theories of Herbert Simon, Arthur F. Bentley, and Harold Lasswell, together with a final essay by Leo Strauss. Perhaps the most important statement by a leading critic of positivism is Leo Strauss's *Natural Right and History* (Chicago: University of Chicago Press, 1953). See also Erich Voegelin's highly polemical essay, *The New Science of Politics* (Chicago: University of Chicago Press, 1952).

Chapter Ten, "Choosing Policies: Strategies of Inquiry and Decision," is a fearfully brief treatment of a highly complex subject. The nature of scientific thought and the special characteristics of the social or human sciences are entire subjects in themselves. A brief description of "two main traditions in science and in the philosophy of scientific method: the aristotelian and the galilean" will be found in the opening chapter of Georg Henrik von Wright, *Explanation and Understanding* (Ithaca, N.Y.: Cornell University Press, 1971); von Wright himself is in the Aristotelian tradition. Unfortunately, the remaining chapters are formidable and not accessible to the neophyte who is unprepared for hard, close, difficult reasoning.

Perhaps the most important work in the "Galilean" or positivist tradition is that of Carl. G. Hempel, whose numerous seminal essays are contained in *Aspects of Scientific Explanation* (New York: Free Press, 1965, 1970). A brief and more elementary statement is his *Philosophy of Natural Science* (Englewood Cliffs, N.J.: Prentice-Hall, 1966). A philosopher of great influence in the philosophy of science is Karl R. Popper, some of whose essays are found in *Objective Knowledge, An Evolutionary Approach* (Oxford: Clarendon Press, 1972). A more accessible source is Brian Magee, *Karl Popper* (New York: Viking, 1973).

For the controversy over the nature of the social sciences in general, and political science in particular, Moon's discussion in volume 1 of the *Handbook* is the best place to begin. By using the footnotes cited there and the bibliography as a starting point, the assiduous reader would gain a fair grasp of the issues and the varying perspectives.

Volume 6 of the *Handbook* is concerned with Policies and Policy making. Other sources include Austin Ranney, ed., *Political Science and Public Policy* (Chicago: Markham, 1968), Richard I. Hofferbert, *The Study of Public Policy* (Indianapolis: Bobbs-Merrill, 1974), Ira Sharkansy and Donald Van Meter, *Policy and Politics in American Governments* (New York: McGraw-Hill Book Co., 1975) and William B. Gwyn and George C. Edwards, III, eds., *Perspectives on Policy Making* (New Orleans: Tulane Univ., 1975).

INDEX

Aquinas, Thomas, 134
Agitator, as personality type, 122–26
American society, de Toqueville on, 8
Americans, and ideology, 63
Aristotle, 1–3, 20, 25, 26, 68, 100
  on change, 66–67
  classification scheme, 70–71
  and cooperation, 59
  and foreign relations, 65
  on government, 10
  and unequal power, 58
Atlanta, study of, 34n
Authority:
  Aristotle on, 1–2
  defined, 25, 26
  and ideology, 61
  and legitimacy, 60
  and politics, 3, 4
Autonomy, 83
  and influence, 40–41

Banks, Arthur S., 90–91
Barber, James D., 126–27
Benedict, Ruth, 57
Bentham, Jeremy, 114

Canada, 65, 66
Capitalism, 18, 19
  defined, 4–5
Causation, 37–41
Change, 66–67, 82, 88
China, People's Republic of, 65
Civil War, U.S., 51, 52, 78

Class:
  ruling, 54–55, 58
  working, 78, 88
Communist Manifesto (Marx), 58
Coercion, 59
  as form of influence, 48–51
  and rational persuasion, 51–53, 83–85
  See also Conflict; Force
Conflict, 59–60
  causes, 76–78
  and inequality of resources, 92–96
  levels of, 85–87
  severity of, 78–80
  and socioeconomic levels, 89
Consensus, 59–60
Constitutional Convention, U.S., 52
Constitutions, 1, 2
Control, 50, 83
  by training, 44, 45
  problems of definition, 25
  reciprocal vs. unilateral, 85
  See also Coercion
Cultural pluralism, 98–99
Culture, political, 121, 125

Dahrendorf, Ralf, 26n
Data, quantitative vs. qualitative, 143–45
Decision making strategies, 129–30
  experimental, 146–47
  holistic, 144–45
  limited responsibility, 145–46
Definitions, 17–19

Democracy, 18, 19, 81n, 92, 99, 121
and change, 67
defined, 4–5
and legitimacy, 60–61
in United States, 61
Dictatorship, defined, 4–5
Discourse of the Origins of Inequality
(Rousseau), 58

Economics, 4, 20
Economic systems, 4–5, 7
Education, 74, 75
Elites, 76
Empirical analysis (*see* Political analysis, empirical
Engels, F., 58
Equality, 76, 92–96
Ethics, 133n

Force, physical, 10–11, 49, 51
Foreign relations, and political systems, 64–66
France, 19n
Freud, Sigmund, 114
Friedrich, Carl J., 31

Germany, 8
Government, 3, 9–10
of agricultural societies, 93
and conflict, 59–60
defined, 8–9
differences, 80–81
popular, 121
Greeks, 10, 23, 51, 64–65, 102
Guerrilla warfare, 51
Gurr, T. R., 95n

Harrington, James, 93–95
Hegemony, 82–99
Hobbes, Thomas, 59, 113, 114, 135
Hofstadter, Richard, 124
Holistic strategies, of decision making, 144–45

Ideology, 98
and legitimacy, 61–64
and personality, 122
Inducement, 45–47
Influence, 3n, 23, 60
and autonomy, 40–41
differences in, 37–39, 83–85
evaluating forms of, 50–53
forms of, 42–50
manifest vs. implicit, 30–32
measuring amounts of, 32–36
observing, 36–37
problems of definition, 25–26, 29

Influence (*cont.*)
and socioeconomic status, 110–11
Information, inundation of, 68–72
Institutions, 87
International Political Science Association, 70
International relations, 51
Intuitionism, 134, 141
Italy, 19n

Jackson, Andrew, 9
Jefferson, Thomas, 9, 95
Johnson, Lyndon, 9

Kant, Immanuel, 134
Knowledge, as resource, 74, 75

Land, as resource, 75, 76
Landtman, Gunnar, 58
Language, 77, 136
Lasswell, Harold, 2–3, 115–17, 122, 123
Law, 20
Leaders, political, 22–23, 127
defined, 58–59
and ideology, 61–64
and legitimacy, 60–61
in polyarchy and hegemony, 83–99
Legislatures, 87
Legitimacy, 60–61
Lenin, 19
Lenski, Gerhard, 93n
Lincoln, A., 9, 124–25
Literacy, 74

Machiavelli, 26, 119, 135
Madison, James, 22
Man, as political animal, 100–104
Marx, 58, 67, 76–78, 114
Mayhew, David R., 36–37
Meaning, analysis of, 15, 136
Measurement, problems of, 141–43
Michels, Roberto, 54
Mill, John Stuart, 135
Mills, Wilbur, 31, 32, 48
Models, mathematical, 130
Modernity, 89–92
degrees of, 72–74
stages of, 92–96
Mosca, Gaetano, 54, 58, 61
Motivation, 4
and power, 56–57, 115–17

Nagel, Jack H., 30, 34
Naturalism, philosophy of, 133–34, 137, 141
Nazis, 16
Negotiator, personality type, 122–26